Ever Wonder Why

和英対訳

誰かに話したくなる「世の中のなぜ?」

ニーナ・ウェグナー=著

IBCパブリッシング

装　　　幀 = 岩目地英樹（コムデザイン）
イラスト = テッド・高橋
翻訳協力 = 中溝俊哉

本書のテキストは、弊社から刊行された英文快読シリーズ
『意外と知らない世の中の「なぜ？」』から転載しています。

小さな疑問が大きな感動へとつながる
「世の中の未知」との遭遇

　人は物心ついた頃から、"世の中の謎"との遭遇がはじまります。
　「空が青いのはなぜ？」
　「なぜ人は笑ったり、泣いたりするのかな？」
　「怖い夢を見て目が覚めると、汗をかいているのはなぜ？
　　　そもそも、なぜ人は夢を見るの？」
　「どうしてドーナツには穴があいているの？」

　このような"謎"に、本書はお答えします。きっと、今となっては質問することさえ忘れていたような疑問に再び出合うことができるでしょう。また、身近にいるこどもたちに「なぜ？なぜ？」と聞かれながらも、答えに窮している謎が本書の中にあふれているはずです。
　世界中のこどもや大人たちが不思議に思っていることを「文化と習慣」「スポーツ」「人のからだ」「自然と動物」「食べ物」の５章にジャンル分けし、自分が気になっていた謎にたどり着くことができるように構成しました。
　また、英語と日本語の対訳になっているので、人類共通の永遠の謎を世界中の人たちと楽しむことができます。あなたの回答に、みんながスッキリした顔をし、握手を求めてくることでしょう。あるいは、あなたが考えもしなかったような謎を問いかけられ、その回答の面白さに、こんどはあなたの方が感動することがあるかもしれません。
　男女長幼を問わず、世界中の人たちが本書によって楽しいコミュニケーションのひとときを持ち、世の中の謎がすこしでも解明されることを希ってやみません。

Contents
目次

小さな疑問が大きな感動へとつながる
「世の中の未知」との遭遇 3

Culture and Tradition
文化と習慣

- Why do people shake hands when they first meet? 14
  わたしたちは初めての人と会うとき、どうして握手をするの？

- Why do people wear their wedding ring on the third finger of the left hand? 16
  なぜ左手の薬指に結婚指輪をつけるの？

- Why do brides wear veils? 18
  どうして花嫁はベールを被るの？

- Why do baby boys wear blue and baby girls wear pink? 20
  なぜ男の赤ちゃんには青い服、女の赤ちゃんには
  ピンクの服を着せるの？

- Why are traffic lights red, yellow, and green? 22
  なぜ信号の色は赤・黄・青(緑)なの？

- How did shaking the head come to mean "no" and nodding the head come to mean "yes"? 26
  どうして頭を横に振ると「いいえ」で、
  前後にうなずくと「はい」の意味になるの？

- Where does the heart shape come from? 28
  ハートの形はどこから来たの？

Contents 目次

- **Where does the hand sign for "peace" come from?** *32*
  「ピース」サインはどこから来たの？
- **Why does Santa Claus wear red and white?** *36*
  サンタクロースの衣装はどうして赤と白なの？
- **Where do high heels come from?** *38*
  ハイヒールはどうしてできたの？
- **Why do only men wear neckties?** *42*
  どうして男の人だけがネクタイを締めるの？
- **Why do chefs wear tall, white hats?** *46*
  どうしてシェフは背の高い白い帽子を被っているの？
- **Why do men usually have
  short hair and women have long hair?** *48*
  どうしてふつう男の人の髪は短くて女の人の髪は長いの？
- **Who wrote the song, "Happy Birthday to You"?** *50*
  だれが「ハッピーバースデイトゥーユー」の歌を作ったの？
- **Where does the phrase "Say cheese" come from?** *54*
  写真を撮るときどうして「チーズ」って言うの？
- **What does "OK" really stand for?** *56*
  「オーケー」の本当の意味は？
- **Why are so few English words spelled the way they sound?** ... *60*
  英単語のつづりは発音通りのものがほとんどないのはなぜ？
- **Why do playing cards have diamonds, hearts, clubs,
  and spades on them?** *64*
  トランプのカードはどうしてダイヤ、ハート、クラブ、
  そしてスペードになっているの？
- **Where does Valentine's Day come from?** *66*
  バレンタインデーはどうしてできたの？
- **Where does Halloween come from?** *70*
  ハロウィーンの起源は？

❏ Where does the Easter Bunny come from? 72
　イースターのうさぎはどこから来たの？
❏ Why do we decorate trees at Christmas? 74
　クリスマスにはどうして木に飾りをつけるの？

Sports
スポーツ

❏ Where did the Olympic symbol and colors come from? 80
　オリンピックのマークと色にはどんな意味があるの？
❏ Why do golf courses have 18 holes? 82
　ゴルフコースはどうして18番ホールまであるの？
❏ Why do golf balls have all those little holes? 86
　ゴルフボールにはどうして小さなくぼみがついているの？
❏ Why do races have 1st, 2nd, and 3rd places? 88
　競技にはなぜ1等、2等、3等があるの？
❏ Where did the word "soccer" come from? 90
　「サッカー」という呼び名はどこから来たの？
❏ Why are soccer balls black and white? 92
　サッカーボールはなぜ白と黒の模様なの？
❏ Why do referees wear stripes? 94
　なぜ審判は縞模様の服を着るの？
❏ Why are sports trophies usually cups? 98
　スポーツのトロフィーは、なぜカップのかたちをしているの？
❏ Why are tennis balls yellow? 100
　テニスボールはどうして黄色なの？

Contents 目次

- **Why are left-handed pitchers called a "southpaw"?** *102*
  なぜ左利きのピッチャーは「サウスポー」と呼ばれるの？
- **Why are races always run counterclockwise?** *104*
  どうして競走では時計の反対回りに走るの？

The Human Body
人のからだ

- **Why do people float in water?** *110*
  どうして人は水の中で浮くの？
- **How many bones are in a human body?** *112*
  人の体にはいくつの骨があるの？
- **How much human hair grows in a day?** *114*
  人の髪の毛は1日にどれだけ伸びるの？
- **Why do people's teeth chatter when they are scared?** *116*
  どうして人は怖い目にあうと歯がガチガチいうの？
- **Why does eating spicy foods make some people sweat?** *118*
  辛い食べ物を食べるとどうして汗をかくの？
- **Why do humans have body hair?** *120*
  人にはどうして毛が生えているの？
- **Why do fingers and toes wrinkle in water?** *122*
  手や足の指は水に浸けるとどうしてしわができるの？
- **Why do humans dream?** *124*
  どうして人は夢を見るの？
- **Why do humans laugh?** *126*
  どうして人は笑うの？

7

❏ **Why do people cry?** *128*
　どうして人は泣くの？

❏ **Why does hair turn gray?** *130*
　どうして白髪が生えてくるの？

❏ **Why are some people right-handed
　and some people left-handed?** *132*
　どうして右利きや左利きの違いが起きるの？

❏ **Why do people catch more colds in the winter?** *136*
　どうして冬になると風邪をひきやすくなるの？

❏ **Why do we itch?** *138*
　どうしてかゆいと感じるの？

❏ **Why does yawning make other people yawn?** *140*
　どうしてあくびは他人に伝染するの？

❏ **Why do our voices sound so different on recordings?** *142*
　どうして声は録音すると違って聞こえるの？

❏ **Is reading in the dark really bad for your eyes?** *146*
　暗いところで字を読むと目が悪くなるの？

❏ **Why do we sometimes wake up sweating
　when we have a bad dream?** *148*
　こわい夢を見て目が覚めるとなぜ汗をかいていたりするの？

Nature and Animals
自然と動物

❏ **What is the temperature of the sun?** *152*
　太陽の温度は何度なの？

❏ **Why are there 365 days in a year?** *156*
　どうして1年は365日なの？

Contents 目次

- **Why does smoke come from fire?** *158*
  なぜ煙は火のあるところから出てくるの？
- **Why is seawater salty?** *160*
  どうして海の水は塩辛いの？
- **Why is the sky blue?** *162*
  どうして空は青いの？
- **Why are clouds white?** *164*
  なぜ雲は白いの？
- **Why do stars sometimes look like they are blinking?** *166*
  なぜ星は瞬いているように見えることがあるの？
- **Why do tree leaves turn color in autumn?** *168*
  どうして木の葉は秋になると色が変わるの？
- **Why can you hear the ocean when you hold a seashell to your ear?** *170*
  なぜ巻貝を耳に当てると海の音が聞こえるの？
- **Does the color red really anger bulls?** *172*
  赤色は本当に牛を怒らせるの？
- **Why do bats sleep upside down?** *174*
  なぜコウモリは逆さになって眠るの？
- **Do fish ever sleep?** *176*
  魚は眠ることがあるの？
- **Why do cats purr?** *178*
  どうして猫はゴロゴロ言うの？
- **Why do horses have to wear "shoes"?** *180*
  馬はどうして「靴」（蹄鉄）を履かなければいけないの？
- **Why do dogs bury their bones?** *184*
  犬はどうして骨を地面に埋めるの？
- **Why do geese fly in a V formation?** *186*
  なぜガンの群れはV字形になって飛ぶの？

- **Why can parrots talk?** *188*
  オウムはどうして人の言葉を話すの？

- **Why are male animals usually more colorful than the female?** *190*
  なぜ動物の雄は雌よりも派手なの？

- **Do other animals laugh when tickled?** *192*
  動物はくすぐったいと笑うの？

- **Why are dogs' noses wet?** *194*
  どうして犬の鼻はぬれているの？

Food
食べ物

- **Why is Caesar salad called a Caesar salad?** *198*
  なぜシーザーサラダと呼ばれるようになったの？

- **Where did the McDonald's sign come from?** *200*
  マクドナルドのマークはどこから来たの？

- **Why does popcorn pop?** *202*
  ポップコーンはどうしてできるの？

- **Why are M&Ms called M&Ms?** *204*
  M&Msはどうして M&Msと呼ばれるようになったの？

- **Why is a hamburger called a hamburger?** *206*
  ハンバーガーはなぜハンバーガーと呼ばれるようになったの？

- **Why are French fries called French fries?** *208*
  フライドポテトはどうして英語で「フレンチフライ」と呼ばれるの？

- **Why do onions make your eyes water?** *210*
  なぜタマネギを切ると涙が出るの？

Contents　目次

❏ **Why does garlic make your breath smell bad?** *212*
　ニンニクを食べるとどうして息が臭くなるの？

❏ **Why does Swiss cheese have holes in it?** *214*
　スイスチーズにはどうして穴があいているの？

❏ **Why do doughnuts have holes?** *216*
　なぜドーナツには穴があいているの？

❏ **Why do lobsters and crabs turn red when cooked?** *220*
　ロブスターやカニは火を通すとどうして赤くなるの？

❏ **Why are pancakes only eaten for breakfast?** *222*
　パンケーキを食べるのはどうして朝食だけなの？

❏ **Why does salt bring out flavor?** *226*
　食べ物は塩を足すとどうしておいしくなるの？

❏ **Why does eating cold things give you a headache?** *228*
　冷たいものを食べるとなぜ頭が痛くなるの？

Culture and Tradition
文化と習慣

Why do people shake hands when they first meet?

The tradition of shaking hands came ancient Greece. Thousands of years ago, most men carried swords and other weapons for protection. When a man met another man and wanted to show that he meant no harm, he would show them his empty hand.

After that, to make sure that neither man would suddenly reach for his weapon, both men would grasp the other's hand tightly until they felt they could truly trust the other person.

So what about the shake? One commonly believed theory is that the men would shake each other's hands to make sure there were no weapons hidden in their sleeves.

Culture and Tradition 文化と習慣

わたしたちは初めての人と会うとき、どうして握手をするの？

握手をする習慣は古代ギリシャの時代にさかのぼります。数千年前、男たちは身を守るために剣や武器を携帯していました。誰かと会ったとき、相手に敵意がないことを伝えるため、何も持っていない手のひらを相手に見せました。

それから、どちらも突然自分の武器に手を伸ばしたりしないことを確認するために、互いに相手を信頼できると感じるまで、手をきつく握りあったのです。

ではどうして握手のとき手を振るのでしょうか？　手を振るのは、そでの中に武器を隠していないことを確かめるためだという説が有力です。

Why do people wear their wedding ring on the third finger of the left hand?

A long time ago, it was believed that the third finger of the left hand held a vein that went straight to the heart. This vein was called *vena amoris,* or "vein of love" in Latin.

Because of this belief, the people who wrote the rules on weddings thought it would be very suiting for married couples to wear a ring on that finger. They wrote that this represented the couple's never-ending love for each other. Thus, the tradition was born.

Culture and Tradition 文化と習慣

なぜ左手の薬指に結婚指輪をつけるの？

　その昔、左手の薬指には心臓に直結する血管があると信じられていました。この血管は「愛の血管」という意味のラテン語、「ヴェナ・アモリス」と呼ばれていました。

　そのことから、結婚の習わしを決めた人々は、結婚するカップルがその指に指輪をはめるのがとてもよいことだと考えたのです。そしてこの慣習はふたりの永遠の愛を意味するのだと説明したのです。このようにして指輪の習慣は生まれたのです。

Why do brides wear veils?

There are many different opinions of why brides around the world wear veils or cover their face in some way. Some say the practice originated from the idea that brides needed to be protected from evil spirits. The ancient Romans covered their brides with veils the color of fire to scare off evil spirits.

In many cultures, wearing a veil or covering one's head is a symbol of respect for God. In Victorian times, the bride's veil came to take on social meanings as well. The longer, heavier, and more detailed the veil, the higher the social ranking of the bride. Royal brides had the longest veils of all.

Today, the veil has come to be a fashion item for the bride.

Brides are not required to wear a veil on their wedding day, but many choose to wear it as a special accessory that can only be worn on one day of their lives.

Culture and Tradition 文化と習慣

どうして花嫁はベールを被るの？

　花嫁がベールや顔を覆うようなものを被ることについては、世界各地に諸説あります。ある人はこの慣習を花嫁を悪霊から守るためと言います。たとえば、古代ローマでは悪霊を怖がらせるために火の色のベールを花嫁に被せたそうです。

　多くの文化圏では頭部を覆ったり、ベールを被るのは神への敬意をあらわすものだという説明もあります。ビクトリア朝の時代には、花嫁のベールは社会階級を反映すると考えられていました。より長くて重く、よりたくさんの細かな装飾が入ったベールほど、花嫁の社会的地位が高いと考えられたのです。そのため英国王室の花嫁は最長のベールになったと言います。

　今日ではベールは花嫁のファッションアイテムのひとつと考えられるようになりました。

　花嫁は結婚式のときに必ずしもベールを被る必要はありません。でも多くの花嫁は人生のたった一度きりの特別なアクセサリーとしてベールを選ぶようです。

Why do baby boys wear blue and baby girls wear pink?

A long time ago, many people believed that the color blue represented the sky, or the heavens. They also believed that the world was full of devils and evil spirits. These spirits were often thought to gather around the rooms of children, so that they could either enter children's bodies or take them away.

The solution to this problem was to make children wear the color blue, the color of the heavens, which would guard against evil spirits.

In ancient times, most cultures believed it was more important for baby boys to live, so that they could carry on the family name. In this way, it came to be that baby boys were dressed in the color blue to protect them.

Later on, baby girls were also given a color to wear: they were given the color pink, which is often thought of as the color of the rose.

Culture and Tradition 文化と習慣

なぜ男の赤ちゃんには青い服、女の赤ちゃんにはピンクの服を着せるの？

　ずいぶん昔の話ですが、人々はよく青は空や天の色と考えていました。また世の中は悪魔や悪霊で満ちていて、悪霊は子どものいる部屋のまわりに集まってきて、子どもたちの体の中に入って悪さをしたり、どこかに連れて行ってしまうと信じられていました。

　こうした問題への解決策として子どもには天上世界の色である青い色の服を着せて、悪霊たちから守ろうとしたのです。

　大昔、多くの場所で家督を継ぐ男の子が生き残ることこそ大事なことだと考えられていました。それが男の子に青い服を着せて守ろうという行動に表れていると考えられます。

　後に、女の子にも色のついたものを着せようということになり、バラの色を思い起こさせるピンク色があてがわれたのです。

Why are traffic lights red, yellow, and green?

Everywhere around the world, traffic lights are red, yellow, and green. In every country, these colors mean the same thing: stop, slow, and go. This was all started by an American man named Lester Farnsworth Wire, who created the first traffic light in 1912.

At first, Wire's traffic light only had two colors, red and green. He used these colors because they were already being used by ships and trains to mean "stop" and "go." Red was chosen as the color to signal "stop" because the color has a very attention-grabbing affect on the human brain.

People notice the color red right away. The color red also creates feelings of anxiety in many people. It was the perfect color to use as a way to tell people to stop.

Culture and Tradition 文化と習慣

なぜ信号の色は
赤・黄・青(緑)なの?

　世界中のどの地域でも信号機の色は赤と黄と緑と決まっています。どの国でもそれぞれ「止まれ」「ゆっくり」「進め」という同じ意味を持っているのです。これは1912年にアメリカ人のレスター・ファーンズワース・ワイア氏が最初の交通信号機を作ったのが始まりです。

　最初、ワイア氏の信号機は赤と緑の2つの色しかついていませんでした。この2つの色を選んだのは、すでに船舶と鉄道の世界で「止まれ」と「進め」の意味で使われていたためです。赤は脳に働きかけ、人の注意をとても強くひくため「止まれ」の意味として採用されていたのです。

　人は赤という色をただちに認識します。また赤は多くの人にとって不安の気持ちをかき立てるそうです。そのような理由で、赤は人に「止まれ」と注意をうながすのにたいへん適しているのです。

The color green, on the other hand, is a color that usually does not upset the human brain. It is a color that occurs in nature, and it seemed like the right color to mean, "go ahead and continue on."

Later on, as the traffic light became more developed, people realized they needed a sign to prepare drivers to stop. The color yellow was chosen because it was the least similar color to both red and green. It was chosen over the color white because a white light could easily be mistaken for a normal street light at night.

一方、緑は通常人の脳を刺激しません。この色は自然の世界でもよく見られ、この色が「前に進め」とか「続けなさい」と言っているように感じるのです。

後に、信号機がさらに発展するなかで人々は運転手が止まる準備をするための合図が必要だと考えるようになりました。そして赤と緑の両方から最も遠い色である黄色が選ばれたのです。これには白が選ばれそうなところを黄色が勝ち抜いたという経緯があります。なぜなら、白の光は夜、通りでいくらでも見かけることのある普通の明かりの色と容易に見間違えるからです。

How did shaking the head come to mean "no" and nodding the head come to mean "yes"?

In many cultures around the world, people shake their head from side to side to mean "no" and nod their head up and down to mean "yes."

The famous biologist Charles Darwin wondered if this was a universal type of language, and if so, what caused it. He studied this very question and came to realize that the answer might lie in how humans communicate before they learn language.

Darwin found that when babies refuse to eat food, they turn their head away and to the side, basically saying "no." When babies do want food, they extend their head forward in a kind of nodding action.

This led Darwin to think that maybe the shaking and nodding of the head is a type of communication that humans are born with. Therefore these expressions are common all over the world, despite different cultures and languages.

Culture and Tradition 文化と習慣

どうして頭を横に振ると「いいえ」で、前後にうなずくと「はい」の意味になるの？

　世界中の多くの国々において頭を横に振ると「いいえ」を意味し、たてに振ると「はい」を意味します。

　著名な生物学者のチャールズ・ダーウィンは、これが世界共通の言語なのか、そしてもしそうならどうしてそうなったのか興味を抱きました。彼はこの疑問について研究し、人間が言語を学ぶ前にどのようにコミュニケーションを行うのかというところにその答えがあるのではないかと考えるようになりました。

　ダーウィンは、赤ん坊は食べたくないときに顔を横に背けることに気づきました。それはつまり「いやだ」ということを伝えているわけです。そして何かを食べたいとき、首を前の方に伸ばし、それがうなずくような格好になるのです。

　ダーウィンはその発見によって、首を横に振ったりうなずいたりするのは、人が生まれながらに持っている意思伝達の方法だと考えたのです。したがって、この表現はどんなに文化や言語が異なっていても世界中どこでも共通のものになったと考えられます。

Where does the heart shape come from?

You will get different explanations of the origin of the heart shape depending on whom you talk to. One theory says that the heart shape simply came from early scientists and doctors trying to draw a picture of the human heart.

Another theory says the heart shape came from the seed of an African plant called silphium. Although silphium was commonly used as a spice for cooking, people also believed it was an effective form of birth control. Silphium was so important in the African market that coins were produced with a design that was shaped like a Silphium seed and that looked like today's symbol of the heart. Because of its properties as a form of birth control, people related the seed and its shape with sex, and later with love.

Culture and Tradition 文化と習慣

ハートの形はどこから来たの？

　ハートマークの起源は、質問する相手によって答えが違います。ある説によれば、ハートの形は単に昔の学者や医師が人の心臓の絵を描こうとしたときの形から来ているとのことです。

　他の説によればシルフィウムと呼ばれるアフリカの植物の種の形からきているというものもあります。シルフィウムは広く料理のスパイスとして用いられていたのですが、同時に避妊に効果がある形だとも信じられていました。シルフィウムはアフリカの市場では、コインがこの種のような形につくられていたほど重要なものでした。そして、まさにその形は今日知られているハートの形と同じだったのです。この避妊のフォルムという特質もあって、人々はこの種が性的なものを想起させる形と考えるようになり、後には性愛と関連付けられることになったのです。

Still another theory says that the heart shape came from the Catholic Church. In the 17th century, Saint Margaret Mary Alacoque had a famous vision of a heart shape surrounded by thorns. Her vision was interpreted as the heart of Jesus Christ, and it came to symbolize love and loyalty. But this theory is not very popular because many researchers believe the heart shape was around much earlier than the 17th century.

Culture and Tradition 文化と習慣

　また別の説によればハートの形はカトリック教会から来ているとも言われます。17世紀、聖マーガレット・メアリー・アラコックが「いばらが巻かれた心臓」の幻影を見て有名になりました。聖マーガレットの幻視したものはイエス・キリストの心臓であると解釈され、それが愛と忠誠のシンボルとなったのです。でも多くの研究者は心臓の形は17世紀よりも早い時期に出現していると考えているため、この説はあまり広く受け入れられていません。

Where does the hand sign for "peace" come from?

A popular story explains that English archers first started showing their second and third fingers to their French enemies during a war in the 15th century. According to the story, the French would cut off the second and third fingers of captured English archers, because these were the fingers that were used to fit an arrow to a bow.

The archers began showing these fingers to their enemies as a fight sign, as if to say, "You haven't got me yet! I dare you to stop me!" Although this colorful story is very popular, researchers say there is no evidence that the French army really cut off the fingers of Englishmen.

Much later, during World War II, the letter V became a sign for "victory," and Britain's prime minister, Winston Churchill, made the letter V with his hand as a sign of hope and an end to war.

Culture and Tradition 文化と習慣

「ピース」サインはどこから来たの？

　15世紀、戦場でイギリスの射手たちが敵のフランス軍に対して人差し指と中指を立てて見せたという有名なエピソードがあります。この話によればフランス軍は捕虜となったイギリス人射手の人差し指と中指を切り落としたと言われています。その2本の指で矢を弓にひっかけるからです。

　射手は、「負けてたまるか、やれるものならやってみな」と言わんばかりに敵にこの指を見せはじめたのです。このいかにもありそうな話は大変有名なのですが、歴史研究家はフランス人がイギリス軍兵士の指を切ったという歴史的根拠はないと言っています。

　そのずっと後の時代、第二次世界大戦中、イギリスの首相ウィンストン・チャーチルが指でVの字をつくって見せ、希望と戦争の終結の印としたことで、これは「勝利（ビクトリー）」のサインになりました。

A few decades later, US President Richard Nixon used the same V hand sign to signal victory during the Vietnam War. But the American youth who opposed the Vietnam War used the same hand sign while saying "Peace," making it a sign of peace. The hand sign became more popular as a sign for "peace" than "victory," and this is the most common meaning of the hand sign today.

それからしばらく経って合衆国大統領リチャード・ニクソンがベトナム戦争での勝利を願ってやはり指で同様のVサインを見せましたが、ベトナム戦争に反対するアメリカの若者たちは、同じサインを見せながら「ピース（平和を）」と叫んだのです。そのためにこのサインは「勝利」のサインというよりは「平和」のサインへと変化したのです。そして今日も「平和」のサインとして一般的には認識されているのです。

Why does Santa Claus wear red and white?

Everybody knows that Santa Claus wears red and white, but not everybody knows that he was dressed in these colors by the Coca-Cola Company!

Before the 20th century, pictures of Santa Claus (also known as Saint Nicholas) showed him wearing all different colors. But red and white didn't become the official colors of his suit until 1931, when an artist named Haddon Sundblom was hired by the Coca-Cola Company to come up with a winter advertisement.

For the ad, Sundblom decided to draw Santa Claus wearing red and white, which were Coca-Cola's official colors. He also drew Santa Claus drinking a bottle of Coca-Cola. The ad was very popular and traveled all over the world. From then on, Santa Claus came to be known as wearing red and white.

Culture and Tradition 文化と習慣

サンタクロースの衣装はどうして赤と白なの？

　サンタクロースが赤と白の衣装を身にまとっているのは誰でも知るところですが、この色になったいきさつがコカコーラ社のせいだと知る人はそう多くないのではないでしょうか？

　20世紀に入る前、サンタクロース（聖ニコラスとしても知られる）の絵はいろいろな色で描かれていました。赤と白の衣装が正式に認められるようになるのは1931年のことです。この年、ハッドン・サンドブラムという画家がコカコーラ社に雇われて、冬のキャンペーン用の広告を制作したのです。

　この広告でサンドブラムはサンタクロースをコカコーラの企業カラーであった赤と白を身にまとったものとして描くことにしたのです。その絵の中でサンタクロースはコカコーラを飲んでいました。この広告は大変成功して、世界中で展開されました。それからというもの、サンタクロースは赤と白の衣装をまとう人物として知られるようになったのです。

Where do high heels come from?

In modern day, high heels are worn mainly by women. But when they were first created, they were meant for men.

High heels were worn for centuries as a helpful accessory for horseback riding. The heel formed a way for the rider's feet to stay in the stirrups, especially if he needed to stand while riding to fight in a battle. Persian men in the Middle Ages had such shoes because they did most of their fighting on horseback.

During the 17th century, the king of Persia sent a group of representatives to Western Europe, and the high heels that these men wore became very popular all across Europe. They made men look taller and manlier, and eventually, they became the favorite accessory of European noble men.

Culture and Tradition 文化と習慣

ハイヒールはどうしてできたの？

　今日ハイヒールは女性の履くものとして知られています。でも世に出た当初は、男性のためのものとして作られたのです。

　ハイヒールは何世紀もの間、乗馬の際に役立つアクセサリーとして履かれていました。ヒールが馬に乗る人が「あぶみ」と呼ばれる馬具に足を掛けやすいようにデザインされていたのです。特に戦の時、馬上に立って戦わなければならないときにそれは重要でした。中世のペルシャの男たちは馬上でほとんどの戦を戦っていましたからこのようなヒールの高い靴を履いていたのです。

　17世紀になってペルシャの王が西ヨーロッパに使者の一団を派遣したとき、このペルシャの男たちが履いていたハイヒールがヨーロッパ中で非常に話題となりました。ハイヒールを履くと男たちは背が高く見え、またより男らしいと見なされたので、ついにはヨーロッパの貴族にとってお気に入りのアイテムとなったのです。

However, during this same period, European women liked to copy men's fashions, and they began to wear high heels as well. However, wearing high heels while walking was very difficult, and eventually, men give up on wearing high heels. But it stuck around as a female accessory. Today, rather than making people look more manly, high heels are a sign of femininity.

Culture and Tradition 文化と習慣

　ところがこの頃、ヨーロッパの女性は男性のファッションを真似ることが流行になっていましたので、女性たちもハイヒールを履くようになったというわけです。でもハイヒールを履いて歩くのは容易でありません。男性はこの高いヒールの靴を履くのを早々にあきらめたのです。でも女性のファッションアイテムとしてその後も残りました。そして今日では、ハイヒールは男らしさを演出するものではなく、女性らしさのシンボルとなったのです。

Why do only men wear neckties?

Researchers say that neckties are only worn by men because they come from military history. In cultures around the world, such as China, Croatia, and Rome, statues, records, and histories show that soldiers with special honors wore a scarf around their necks to show their high position in the military.

During the 17th century, the King of France saw the scarves worn by the Croatian army and became interested in them. He began to wear scarves too, and they became very popular in France. French fashion designers began to come up with many different types of scarves to be worn around the neck.

The fancy neck scarves of France made their way to England in the late 17th century. It became a popular accessory for rich British men. Early in the 19th century, wearing a cloth tied around the neck became fashionable for men of all classes, and

Culture and Tradition 文化と習慣

どうして男の人だけが
ネクタイを締めるの？

　研究者たちはネクタイを男性だけが身に着ける理由を戦争の歴史から説明しています。中国、クロアチア、ローマといった世界中の文化を見てみると、特別な名誉を与えられた兵士たちが首の周りにスカーフを巻き、軍隊での高い階級を誇示してきたという証拠が、銅像や戦記、歴史の中に残されています。

　17世紀、フランスの王はクロアチア軍の兵隊たちが着けているスカーフを見て興味を持ちました。そして王は自分でもスカーフを着け始め、フランス中でそれが大流行になりました。フランスのファッションデザイナーたちは首の周りに巻くさまざまなタイプのスカーフをこぞってデザインするようになりました。

　首に巻くフランスのおしゃれなスカーフは17世紀末になってイギリスに渡ると、裕福な英国紳士のファッションアイテムとして人気を博しました。19世紀初頭には首の周りに巻く布はすべての社会階級の男性のためのファッションとなり、このアクセサリーは「タイ」と呼ばれるようになりました。1800年代、ナポレ

the accessory began to be called a "tie." Napoleon Bonaparte made a simple black tie very popular among the European military of the 1800s.

During the industrial revolution in the 1900s, people began to work many hours of the day in factories, and they preferred simple clothes to fancy clothes that got in the way of work. Still, men continued to wear ties, although their design became very simple. From then on, the style of ties became simple and clean, like the tie we know today.

Culture and Tradition 文化と習慣

オン・ボナパルトがヨーロッパの軍隊でシンプルな黒いタイを普及させました。

　1900年代の産業革命の頃、人々は工場で長時間労働をし始め、仕事のじゃまにならないように、手の込んだ衣服よりはシンプルな衣服を選びました。デザインは大変簡素化されたものの、男性はネクタイを締め続けました。こうしてネクタイは今日私たちが目にするような簡素ですっきりしたスタイルになったのです。

Why do chefs wear tall, white hats?

In most restaurants, chefs are required to wear a hat of some sort to keep hair from falling into food. But the tall, white hats that we often see professional chefs wearing are special hats called "toques."

The toque comes from France, and their tall shape with a loose top developed over centuries of cooking history. The tall shape of the hat is supposed to draw heat up toward the top, to keep the head of the chef nice and cool.

Toques usually have 100 folds, and these are supposed to represent how many ways an egg can be cooked.

In a kitchen, the chef with the most skill and experience is supposed to have the tallest toque. The hat's white color is thought to be best for showing the cleanliness of the kitchen.

Culture and Tradition 文化と習慣

どうしてシェフは
背の高い白い帽子を被っているの？

　たいていのレストランでシェフたちは髪の毛が食べ物の中に落ちないようになんらかの帽子を被ることが求められています。でもプロのシェフたちはよく「トーク」と呼ばれる白くて背の高い特別な帽子を被っています。

　トークはフランスから来たもので、先端の方がダブダブになっていて背の高いデザインは何世紀もの料理の歴史のなかで発展してきたものです。背が高いのは体温を先端から抜くためのもので、シェフの頭を見た目によく、またクールに保つようになっています。

　トークには通常100の折り目があり、卵でいく通りもの料理ができるということを象徴していると言われています。

　厨房では一番スキルが高く経験のあるシェフが一番背の高いトークを被ることになっています。この帽子の白さは厨房が清潔に保たれていることを示すのに最適な色と考えられています。

Why do men usually have short hair and women have long hair?

Men and women both wore their hair rather long for much of history. Men also wore long beards.

But in the 4th century, Alexander the Great required all of his soldiers to cut their hair and beards so that their enemies couldn't grab them in battle. Then, the Romans also had their men wear their hair short for military reasons.

As time passed, men wearing short hair came to mean all the things that Rome stood for, such as law, order, correctness, and civilization. Long hair became associated with women, wildness, and weakness.

Some of these meanings have held on, even to this day.

Culture and Tradition 文化と習慣

どうしてふつう男の人の髪は短くて女の人の髪は長いの？

　歴史的には実は男性も女性も髪を長く保っていた時代が長いのです。男性はまた長いひげをたくわえていました。
　ところが、4世紀になってアレキサンダー大王が、戦闘中敵につかまれないように兵士に髪と髭を切るように命じました。また古代ローマ人も軍事的な理由から髪を短くしていました。

　時が経つと男性が髪を短く保つことは法律、社会秩序、常識的価値観、そして文明といったローマを象徴するものすべてに関係するようになりました。一方長い髪は「女性」、「野蛮」、そして「弱さ」といったものを連想させるものとなりました。
　こうした意味合いはそのまま引き継がれ現在でも残っているのです。

Who wrote the song, "Happy Birthday to You"?

"Happy Birthday to You" was first written in 1893 by two sisters named Patty and Mildred Hill. Patty was a kindergarten teacher, and her older sister, Mildred, was a skilled pianist and musician.

Patty was bothered by the music that she had to teach at school. The songs were usually too difficult for small children to remember and sing. So she began to work with Mildred to write simple but pleasing songs for children.

Culture and Tradition 文化と習慣

だれが「ハッピーバースデイトゥーユー」の歌を作ったの？

　『ハッピーバースデイトゥーユー』は1893年にパティ・ヒルとミルドレッド・ヒルという姉妹によって書かれました。パティは幼稚園の先生で姉のミルドレッドはピアノの上手な音楽家でした。

　パティは幼稚園で教える音楽の授業が悩みの種でした。歌は小さな子どもたちにとって覚えたり歌ったりするのにむずかしすぎたからです。そこで彼女はミルドレッドと一緒に、子どもたちにも簡単でしかも楽しめる歌を作り始めたのです。

One of the songs the sisters wrote, "Good Morning to All," became very popular with the children. Nobody knows how the words actually got changed to "Happy Birthday to You," but one theory is believed to be true: the children in Patty's class liked the song "Good Morning to All" so much that they would start singing it with different words for all kinds of occasions.

One of the occasions must have been somebody's birthday, and the words "Happy Birthday to You" has stuck until present day.

Culture and Tradition 文化と習慣

　ふたりで書いた歌の中で『みんなにおはよう』という歌は大変子どもたちに人気がありました。この歌がどのようにして『ハッピーバースデイトゥーユー』という替え歌に変わっていったのかは誰にも知るよしがありませんが、パティのクラスの子どもたちは『みんなにおはよう』があまりにお気に入りだったので、いろいろな場面で歌詞を変えて歌ったのがきっかけではないかという説が信じられています。

　そうした場面の中には誰かの誕生日もあったに違いなく、『ハッピーバースデイトゥーユー』が今日まで残ったのだというわけです。

Where does the phrase "Say cheese" come from?

You hear it all the time: before anybody takes a picture, somebody will call out, "Say cheese!" So where did this funny phrase come from, and why do we say it?

Nobody knows for sure who the first person to come up with "Say cheese" was, but people think it started in America in the 1940s. A newspaper article in the *Big Spring Herald* from 1943 told readers that saying the word "cheese" would make it look like they were smiling, so anyone can take a pleasant photo no matter what they're feeling or thinking.

People found this to be a true and useful trick, so it became a tradition, catching on among picture-takers even internationally.

写真を撮るとき
どうして「チーズ」って言うの？

　写真を撮ろうとしているとき、誰かが「チーズ！」と叫ぶのをしょっちゅう聞くのではないでしょうか？ それにしてもこのおかしな言葉はどこから来たのでしょう。そしてなぜそんなことを言うようになったのでしょう？

　誰がそれを言い出したのかはさだかではありませんが、1940年代のアメリカが発祥であると考える人がいます。ビッグスプリングヘラルド紙の1943年に掲載された記事には「チーズ」と声に出して言えば、顔が笑っているように見えると書かれています。だから内心どんなことを感じたり考えたりしていても、出来のいい写真が誰にでも撮れるというわけです。

　次第にみんなはこの新聞の言っていることは本当で便利な方法だと気づき始め、ついには世界中どこでも通用するような伝統になったのです。

What does "OK" really stand for?

"OK" is a little word that can be used almost anywhere in the world and will be instantly understood—but where does it come from? And what do the letters O and K have to do with anything?

It all started in America in the 1830s. It was popular at the time to shorten phrases into abbreviations.

For example, people would use "i.s.b.d." for "it shall be done," or "t.b.d." for "to be determined." But it was an especially fun trick to shorten things into wrong letters that still sounded correct. For example, "all right" was shortened to "o.w.", or "oll write."

Culture and Tradition 文化と習慣

「オーケー」の本当の意味は？

　「OK」は世界中のほとんどどこででも使われていて直ちに意味がわかる短い言葉ですが、その由来は何なのでしょうか？ OとKという文字には一体どんな意味があるのでしょうか。

　それは1830年代のアメリカで生まれました。その頃、いろいろな言い回しを短い省略記号に置き換えるのが流行っていました。

　たとえば、「i.s.b.d.」は it shall be done（終わります）のことだし、「t.b.d.」と言えば、to be determined（後ほど決定）のことです。でも省略した文字を、発音は同じだけれど間違った文字に置き換えるというのも楽しいお遊びだったのです。例をあげると all right は「o.w.」とか「oll write」などに短くされたのです。

One day, a newspaper editor used the abbreviation "o.k." in an article to stand for "all correct." This really took off and gained popularity, but it became an official word when the telegraph was invented. Telegraph messengers used "OK" to mean everything was fine, or "all correct," and the word has stuck around with this meaning ever since.

Culture and Tradition 文化と習慣

　ある日、ある新聞の編集者がall correct（すべて正解）の意味で「o.k.」という省略語を使ったのです。これはまったくのビッグヒットとなり大人気になりました。しかも電信技術が発明されたとき、これが正式な単語として認知されたのです。電報の文面で「OK」が「すべては順調」（すべて正しい）という意味で使われました。そしてそれ以来その意味で誰もが使うようになったのです。

Why are so few English words spelled the way they sound?

Sometimes English spelling doesn't seem to make any sense: why is there a "gh" in "eight"? Why is there a "b" in "lamb"? Why is there a "k" in "know"? It's enough to drive a person crazy!

The answer can be found in the history of the English language and the history of the printing press. When England was first starting to print books in the 15th century, there were some big changes happening in spoken English. Middle English was changing into Modern English, and people were pronouncing things differently all the time.

In Middle English, the "gh" in "eight" and the "k" in "know" were actually pronounced. So were a lot of other letters that are silent in English today. So, by the time book printers had finished figuring out how to spell English words, a lot of words no longer sounded like the way they were spelled.

Culture and Tradition 文化と習慣

英単語のつづりは発音通りのものが
ほとんどないのはなぜ？

　英語の綴りってまったく不合理だと思うことはありませんか？　なぜ"eight"には"gh"が入っていたり、"lamb"には"b"が付いているのだろうとか、"know"にはどうして"k"が付いているのだろうとか……もうそんなこと考え始めると頭がおかしくなりますね。

　この謎の答えは英語や活字印刷の歴史をひも解くとわかります。英国が初めて本の印刷を始めた15世紀、非常に大きな変化が英語の話し言葉に起こったのです。中世英語と呼ばれる当時の英語は現代英語に変わりつつあり、人々の英語の発音もどんどん変わっていったのです。

　中世英語では"eight"の"gh"や"know"の"k"などは実際に発音されていたのです。今日「黙字」といって発音されない他の多くの文字でも同様でした。それで印刷業者がどのように英単語をスペルするのか決めた頃には実際の発音は綴りとは異なるものになってしまっていたのです。

At around the same time, the Normans invaded England, and French royalty took over England. They brought many French words, which are full of silent letters (such as the "t" in "ballet"), into the English vocabulary.

Culture and Tradition 文化と習慣

　同時期、ノルマン人がイギリスの地を侵略し、フランスの王族がイギリスを支配していました。彼らはたくさんの発音しない文字（balletのtなどがそうです）を含むフランス語の単語を英語にもたらしたというわけです。

Why do playing cards have diamonds, hearts, clubs, and spades on them?

It is commonly believed that the diamonds, hearts, clubs, and spades that make up the suits of playing cards came from 14th century France. One theory is that the different suits represented the four classes of French society.

The hearts are thought to have represented royalty and the upper class. Diamonds are thought to represent the middle class because many shopkeepers of the time used diamond-shaped shop signs. Spades represent the military because the spade is shaped like a sword, and clubs represent the poor class, because it is shaped like a clover, a type of plant that grows in country fields.

Culture and Tradition 文化と習慣

トランプのカードはどうしてダイヤ、ハート、クラブ、そしてスペードになっているの?

　ダイヤ、ハート、クラブ、スペードというマーク(スートと呼びます)は14世紀のフランスから来たトランプのセットが起源だと言われています。ある説によればこれらの異なるスートはフランス社会の4つの階級を反映しているとのことです。

　ハートは王族や貴族を意味し、ダイヤはその時代の多くの商人たちがダイヤのマークを付けた店を経営していたため彼らの属する中流階級を意味していたと考えられています。スペードは剣の形をしているので騎士階級を、そしてクラブは田舎の農園でよく見かけるクローバーのような形をしているので貧困層を表しているのです。

Where does Valentine's Day come from?

Valentine's Day is named after Saint Valentine, a holy figure in the Catholic Church. But there are three different Saint Valentines, and nobody is sure which Saint Valentine February 14th is named after.

One Saint Valentine was a priest in Rome in the third century. The Emperor of Rome at the time decided that unmarried men made better soldiers than men with wives and children, so he outlawed young men to marry. Valentine thought this was unfair, so he continued to perform secret marriages for young lovers. When the emperor found out, he put Valentine to death.

Culture and Tradition 文化と習慣

バレンタインデーは どうしてできたの？

　バレンタインデーはカトリック教会における聖人の聖バレンタインにちなんで名付けられています。実は聖バレンタインは3人いるのですが、2月14日がどのバレンタインから来たのかはわかっていません。

　ひとりのバレンタインは3世紀のローマで司祭をしていました。その時のローマ皇帝は未婚の男性は妻や子どものいる者よりもすぐれた兵隊になると考え、若い男性が結婚することを法律で禁じたのです。バレンタインはこれは不当なことだと考え、愛し合う若者たちを秘密裏に結婚させ続けたのです。でも皇帝がそれを見つけ出し、バレンタインは死刑になったのです。

Another Saint Valentine is thought to be a man named Valentine who was in prison. He fell in love with a young woman while in jail—perhaps the jail keeper's daughter. According to the story, he sent this woman a letter before he was put to death. He signed this letter, "From your Valentine." Some people believe that's where the phrase "Be my Valentine" comes from.

Culture and Tradition 文化と習慣

　もうひとりの聖バレンタインは牢屋に入れられていたバレンタインと呼ばれる男であると考えられています。彼は牢にいたとき、おそらく獄吏の娘と思われる若い女性と恋に落ちました。この言い伝えによれば、バレンタインは死刑になる前にこの女性に手紙を送ったそうです。そして「あなたのバレンタインより」と署名したのです。これが「わたしのバレンタインになってくれますか」というフレーズの起源だというわけです。

Where does Halloween come from?

The first people to celebrate Halloween were the Celts, a group of people who lived in Europe about 2,000 years ago. For the Celts, November 1st was the official end of summer, and they called it "All Hallows Day." The day before that, October 31st, was called "All Hallow's Eve," or "Halloween" for short.

On Halloween, the tradition in Scotland and Ireland was to dress up and carry lamps made out of turnips. When Scottish and Irish people came to the United States, they brought their Halloween traditions, but instead of turnips, they used pumpkins for their lamps. This is where jack-o-lanterns come from.

During the holiday, people would offer food to dead spirits. This tradition changed over time to giving food to the poor. Then this tradition changed to giving food to children who were dressed up. This is where trick-or-treating comes from.

Culture and Tradition 文化と習慣

ハロウィーンの起源は？

　ハロウィーンを最初に祝った人々はおよそ2000年前にヨーロッパで暮らしていたケルト人です。ケルトの人々にとって11月1日は夏の終わりの日と定められていて、「オール・ハローズ・デー」と呼ばれていました。その前日である10月31日は「オール・ハローズ・イブ」、あるいは短く「ハロウィーン」と呼ばれたのです。

　ハロウィーンの日、伝統的にスコットランドとアイルランドでは皆が着飾りカブで作ったランプを持って出掛けました。スコットランドとアイルランドの人々が合衆国にわたった時、ハロウィーンの伝統も持ち込みました。ただし、ランプにはカブの代わりにカボチャを使ったのです。これが「ジャック・オ・ランタン」の由来です。

　この休日の間、人々は亡くなった人の魂に向けて食べ物を供えました。これが時を経て貧しい人々に施しをする習慣に変わったのです。さらにこれが着飾った子どもたちに食べ物をあげる習慣になりました。これが「トリック・オア・トリート」の由来です。

Where does the Easter Bunny come from?

Originally, Easter was the celebration of spring, new life, and fertility. The egg and the rabbit were common symbols of these ideas. But the Easter Bunny first appears in German literature in the 1600s. In the story, a rabbit named Oschter Haws lays a nest full of colorful eggs for good children.

The Oschter Haws story gained popularity, and German bakeries began to make rabbit-shaped Oschter Haws sweets. When German and Dutch people began to move to the United States in the 1700s, they brought the story of Oschter Haws with them.

With time, the story was changed to the rabbit bringing chocolates and sweets to good children, and the tradition caught on.

Culture and Tradition 文化と習慣

イースターのうさぎは
どこから来たの？

イースターとは元来、春、新しい命、そして豊穣のお祝いです。卵やうさぎというのはこれらを象徴するものとして広く知られています。でもイースターのうさぎは1600年代にドイツの文学に最初の記録が残っています。その話によればオシュター・ハウズと呼ばれるうさぎが、よい子どもたちのために色とりどりの卵で巣をいっぱいにするのです。

このオシュター・ハウズの物語は人気が出て、ドイツのパン屋さんがうさぎの形をしたオシュター・ハウズのスイーツを作り始めました。1700年代にドイツ人とオランダ人の移民が合衆国に来たとき、彼らはオシュター・ハウズの話をもたらしました。

時とともに話は変化していき、うさぎがチョコレートやスイーツをよい子たちに運んでくるという話になり、その習わしが人気を博したのでした。

Why do we decorate trees at Christmas?

The tradition of bringing green branches and leaves into the house during the cold, bare, winter months existed in several cultures throughout the world, including Rome and Egypt.

Having the pieces of green inside the house reminded people that spring and new life would be coming soon. They were nice ideas, and many Christians started to use this practice as a way to represent Jesus Christ's birth. This was the earliest version of a Christmas tree.

But the practice of decorating a Christmas tree did not happen until the 1600s in Livonia and Germany. Historical records say that in Livonia, people would cut down a tree, decorate it, and take it into the town square where people would sing and dance around it.

Culture and Tradition 文化と習慣

クリスマスには
どうして木に飾りをつけるの？

　草木も茂らない寒い冬の数ヵ月の間に、緑の木の枝や葉を家の中に持ち込むという習慣はローマやエジプトといった世界のいくつかの文明圏で存在していました。

　家の中に緑を持ち込むことは、春や新しい命がほどなく戻ってくることを人々に思い起こさせます。これはいいアイデアに思えたので、多くのキリスト教徒がイエス・キリストの誕生を象徴する方法として、この習慣を実践し始めたのでした。これはクリスマスツリーの最も初期のバージョンと言えるでしょう。

　でもクリスマスツリーを飾りつけることはリボニア（ラトビア、エストニア両共和国の占める地方）とドイツで1600年代になるまでは行われませんでした。歴史文書によると、リボニアの人々は木を切り倒してそれを飾りたて、街の広場に持ち込み、木の周りで歌い踊ったとあります。

In the 18th century, people in North Germany started decorating Christmas trees with candles. People say this idea came from Martin Luther, who was walking home one winter night and saw the stars shining through the branches of a tree. It was a beautiful image and he went home to tell his family about it. The family tried to create a similar image by decorating a tree with candles.

This practice caught on and spread to other European countries. Even to this day, we decorate Christmas trees with little lights.

Culture and Tradition 文化と習慣

　18世紀、北ドイツの人々がろうそくを使ってクリスマスツリーを飾り始めました。これを着想したのはマルチン・ルターだと言われています。ルターは冬の夜、歩いて自宅に帰っていると、ある木の枝の隙間から星々が輝いているのを見たのです。それがとてもきれいだったので、帰宅した彼はその様子を家族に話しました。ルターの家族はろうそくで木を飾ってそれを再現しようとしたのです。

　そしてこの習わしが流行し、ヨーロッパ各国に波及したのです。そして現在でもクリスマスツリーは小さな電球で飾られるわけです。

Sports
スポーツ

Where did the Olympic symbol and colors come from?

The symbol of the Olympic games is five interlocking rings of five different colors on a white background. The design was created in 1912 by Baron Pierre de Coubertin, who helped found the modern Olympic games.

The reason why de Coubertin used blue, yellow, black, green, and red on a white background is because these were all the colors that were used on the flags of all the countries that participated in the Olympic games that year.

The idea for the five rings came from de Coubertin's earlier work as the man in charge of USFSA, an early French sports association. The symbol for the USFSA was two interlocking rings, which represented unity among humanity.

Sports スポーツ

オリンピックのマークと色にはどんな意味があるの？

　オリンピックの旗のマークは白地に5色の輪が互いに連結し合ったものです。このデザインは1912年に近代オリンピック競技の創設に尽力したピエール・ド・クーベルタン男爵によって作られたものです。

　クーベルタン男爵が青、黄、黒、緑、赤を白地に用いたのは、それらがその年のオリンピック競技に参加した国が国旗として使っている色のすべてだったからです。

　五輪のモチーフは、USFSAというフランスのスポーツ協会に関わっていたクーベルタン男爵の以前の作品が元になっています。USFSAの旗は2つの連結した輪で、「人類の統合」を象徴していたといいます。

Why do golf courses have 18 holes?

For a long time, the number of holes in a golf course was different from course to course. But in the mid-eighteenth century, the St. Andrews Society of Golfers in St. Andrews, Scotland, decided that 18 would be the standard number of holes.

Because St. Andrews was known as the best golf club at the time, all other golf courses copied St. Andrews and decided they would also offer 18 holes. Over time, this became the required number of holes on a golf course.

At first, St. Andrews offered just 12 holes on their course, and they all took the players away from the clubhouse. Because it was not fun to simply walk back to the clubhouse after a round of golf, players usually played the same 12 holes going the opposite direction, all the way back to the clubhouse.

Sports スポーツ

ゴルフコースはどうして18番ホールまであるの？

　ゴルフコースのホール数は長いあいだコースによって異なっていました。ところが18世紀半ば、スコットランドのセント・アンドリュースにあるセント・アンドリュース・ゴルファー協会が18ホールを標準とする決定をしました。

　当時この協会が最良のゴルフクラブとして知られていたため、他のゴルフコースもセント・アンドリュースを真似て18ホールのコースを提供することにしたのです。時が経つにつれてこれがゴルフコースにとって必須のホール数になっていったのです。

　最初、セント・アンドリュースには12ホールしかなく、プレイが進むとプレイヤーはどんどんクラブハウスから離れていってしまいます。12ホール分プレイして、そのまま歩いて帰ってくるのはつまらないので、プレイヤーたちは同じ12ホールを逆にプレイしながらクラブハウスに戻ってくるわけです。

But because each tee was right next to a hole, the players really only had 11 holes to play going both ways. This meant that a full round of golf going from and back to the clubhouse was 22 holes.

Then St. Andrews decided that the distance between the first four holes was too close together. To solve this problem, they got rid of two holes. This made the total number of holes going one way nine, making it 18 holes total.

Finally, St. Andrews came up with the idea of arranging the 18 holes in a way that would make players circle from the clubhouse all the way back. This became the standard, and golf courses are still built this way today.

でもそうすると、各ティーはホールのすぐ隣ですから、実際に往復でプレイするのは11ホール分だということになります。ということは、フルにラウンドをプレイしながら行って帰ってくると合計22ホール分ということになるのです。

それからセント・アンドリュースは、最初の4ホールの間隔が近すぎるとの結論を出しました。この問題を解決するために、2ホールが取り除かれました。これで一方向のホール数が9つとなり、計18ホールとなったのです。

ついにセント・アンドリュースはクラブハウスからプレイを開始してプレイヤーたちが18ホールをぐるっと廻りながら戻ってくるというコースを考案したのです。これが標準となり、ゴルフコースは今日でもこのように設計されているのです。

Why do golf balls have all those little holes?

Golf balls used to be totally smooth. But one day, golf players noticed that old golf balls with little cuts and scratches flew the best through the air. So it became common practice to only play with old golf balls.

Later, a scientist studied the reason why old golf balls with cuts worked better. He found out that the cuts and scratches created better flow of air around the ball, which made the ball fly farther and straighter.

With this new knowledge, golf ball makers started to put little holes on the golf balls on purpose. They put the holes all over the ball so that they would separate the air around it evenly on all sides.

Sports スポーツ

ゴルフボールにはどうして小さなくぼみがついているの？

　ゴルフボールは以前は完全に表面が滑らかでした。でもあるときゴルフプレイヤーたちは小さなカットや傷が生じている古いゴルフボールの方が風を切ってよく飛ぶことに気がつきました。それで古いゴルフボールを使ってプレイするのが一般的になったのでした。

　後にある科学者が古くて切り込みのあるゴルフボールの方がなぜよく飛ぶのか、その原因を究明しました。すると、切れ込みや傷がボールの周りの空気の流れを良くし、より遠くに、より真っすぐに飛ぶことを発見したのです。

　この新たな発見により、ゴルフボールの製造メーカーはわざとゴルフボールの表面に小さな穴をつけるようになったのです。小さな穴をボールの表面全体に設けることによって、ボールのあらゆる側からでも均等に、空気を分離させることができるようになったのです。

Why do races have 1st, 2nd, and 3rd places?

One day in the early seventeenth century, an official of Chester, England, was asked to prepare for a horse race. The official agreed to give a silver trophy to the winner of the race, and he set out to hire a silversmith to make a trophy.

The silversmith he hired made the trophy, but the official thought the finished product was not quite right. He asked the silversmith to make another trophy. When the smith showed the second trophy to the official, it was still not right. So the smith made a third trophy, which was finally what the official was looking for.

The official now had three trophies instead of one. He did not want to waste the valuable silver, so he decided to give the trophies to the people who came in first, second, and third place.

Sports スポーツ

競技にはなぜ
1等、2等、3等があるの？

　17世紀初頭のある日、イギリスはチェスターのある役人が競馬を開催するように依頼されました。彼は勝者に銀のトロフィーを授与することに同意し、トロフィーを作るよう銀細工師をひとり雇いました。

　この銀細工師は確かにトロフィーを作りましたが、できあがったものはこの役人の意にかなわないものでした。そこで役人はこの銀細工師にもうひとつトロフィーを作らせました。

細工師は2つめのトロフィーを見せたのですが、役人はそれでも満足しませんでした。そこで細工師は3つめのトロフィーを作ったところ、ようやくその役人の期待したものができたのです。

　この役人はいまやひとつではなく3つのトロフィーを持っています。彼はこの貴重な銀を無駄にしたくなかったので、1着、2着、3着でレースを終えた者たちにこのトロフィーを授与することにしたのでした。

Where did the word "soccer" come from?

Much of the world calls the sport "football," so where did the word "soccer" come from?

The word "soccer" comes from the British. The game we know today as soccer was first played in England by the rich, upper classes. These people called the game "soccer." When the game became more popular with the poorer classes, the game began to be called "football."

However, when the sport started to be played abroad, there were many other countries, such as the United States, Canada, Ireland, and South Africa, that already had a different game called "football." In these countries, the word "soccer" was used.

Sports スポーツ

「サッカー」という呼び名はどこから来たの？

　世界中の多くの地域でこのスポーツは「フットボール」と呼ばれるのですが、ではどのように「サッカー」という単語は生まれたのでしょうか？

　サッカーという単語はイギリスから来ました。今日サッカーとして知られている競技はイギリスで裕福な上流階級の人々が行っていました。そして競技を始めた人々が「サッカー」と呼んだのです。この競技が下流階級の人々のあいだでも人気になったとき、人々はこれを「フットボール」と呼び始めました。

　ところが、このスポーツが合衆国、カナダ、アイルランド、そして南アフリカなど、イギリス以外の国々でも行われるようになったとき、「フットボール」という名で行われる別の競技がすでに存在していたのです。こうした国々で「サッカー」という呼び名が使われたのです。

Why are soccer balls black and white?

The 1970 FIFA World Cup in Mexico was the first time a black-and-white soccer ball was used. The ball was created by Adidas and called the Telstar.

In the 1970s, most televisions were black-and-white, so the black-and-white pattern of the ball was created to help viewers see the ball better on television.

It became a tradition to use the Telstar ball at all World Cups until 2006. Now independent soccer leagues and World Cups use different kinds of balls, but many still prefer the Telstar as the best soccer ball.

サッカーボールはなぜ白と黒の模様なの？

1970年のメキシコでのFIFAワールドカップで黒白のサッカーボールが初めて使われました。このボールはアディダスが作ったもので、テルスターと呼ばれました。

1970年代、まだほとんどのテレビは白黒だったので、テレビ画像として観戦者が観やすい黒と白の模様がボールに付けられたのです。

2006年のワールドカップまではこのテルスターを使うのが伝統とされていました。現在、独立系のサッカー連盟やワールドカップは異なる種類のボールを使っていますが、今でもテルスターは一番人気のサッカーボールとされています。

Why do referees wear stripes?

Referees have to wear clothing that sets them apart from players to avoid confusion on the playing field. While some referees in some sports wear bright colors, the referees of most North American sports wear black and white stripes. This tradition is believed to have been started by a referee from Michigan.

Sports スポーツ

なぜ審判は縞模様の服を着るの？

　審判員は競技場でプレイヤーたちと混乱しないよう、見分けがつきやすい服を着ることが決められています。ある種のスポーツにおいて審判員は明るい色を着る一方で、北米のほとんどのスポーツの審判員は白黒の縞模様を着用しています。この習慣はミシガン州出身のある審判員によって始められたと信じられています。

Lloyd Olds was a referee for high school and college sports, and he usually wore a white shirt to games. During one football game in 1920, one of the teams also wore white shirts and the quarterback of the white-shirt team handed the ball to Olds by mistake. At this point he knew he needed another uniform so such mistakes would never happen. Olds came up with the idea of wearing stripes, and he had his friend make him a black-and-white striped shirt.

He wore the shirt to a basketball game in 1921 and other referees thought this uniform was a good idea. They also started to wear striped shirts, and eventually, it became tradition.

Sports スポーツ

　ロイド・オールズ氏は高校や大学のスポーツの審判員で、競技ではいつも白いシャツを着ていました。1920年に行われたあるフットボール競技で、ひとつのチームが同じような白いシャツを着ていたために、そのチームのクォーターバックは間違ってボールをオールズに渡してしまいました。この時点で彼は、このようなミスが二度と起こらないように別のユニフォームが必要だと思いました。オールズ氏は縞のシャツを着るというアイデアを思いつき、友人に頼んで白黒のストライプ模様のシャツを作ったのです。

　彼は1921年にあるバスケットボールの試合でこのシャツを着ていたら、他の審判員たちもそのユニフォームはとてもいいアイデアだと感じたのです。そこで彼らはストライプ模様のシャツを着るようになり、やがては習慣となったのです。

Why are sports trophies usually cups?

Although there are several theories, the oldest possible origin of a cup used as a trophy can be found in ancient Greek literature. In the *Iliad*, the Greek poet Homer describes the famous hero Achilles as honoring his dead friend with a festival of sports.

Some of the prizes for these sports were different kinds of cups, such as a vase and a large bowl with two handles. Later in history, the first winner of the men's 200-meter race in the ancient Greek Olympics was given 100 vases of olive oil.

Some say that over time, this tradition of giving bowls and other vessels turned into the cups we see today at sporting events like the World Cup, Stanley Cup, and the Wimbledon trophy.

Sports スポーツ

スポーツのトロフィーは、なぜカップのかたちをしているの？

　これにはいくつかの説があるのですが、トロフィーとしてカップを用いたおそらく最古の起源は、古代ギリシャの文学の中に見出せるそうです。ギリシャの詩人ホメロスは、叙事詩『イーリアス』の中で、有名な英雄アキレスが亡くなった友人の名誉をたたえるためにスポーツの祭典を行ったと記しています。

　この競技の賞の中には、壺形のものや2つの取手のついた鉢形のものなど、異なる形をしたカップがありました。後に、古代ギリシャのオリンピックの男子200メートル走の勝者に100壺のオリーブオイルが授与されたという記録があります。

　ある説によると、時が経つにつれ、鉢や杯を与えるこの伝統がワールドカップ、スタンレーカップ、そしてウィンブルドンのような今日のスポーツイベントで見られるようなカップに変化したそうです。

Why are tennis balls yellow?

Tennis balls are a special color of yellow because it is believed that it is easier to see, not just for the players, but also for fans watching on television.

Some say that orange is actually an easier color to see, but orange does not show up well on television.

For this reason, all professional tennis matches use yellow balls.

Sports スポーツ

テニスボールはどうして黄色なの？

　テニスボールは特別な黄色をしていますが、それはテニスをプレイする人にもそうですが、ゲームをテレビ観戦しているファンにもよく見えると信じられているからです。

　中にはオレンジ色のほうが実はよく見えるのだと言う人もいますが、それだとテレビ画面上ではあまりよく見えないのです。

　こうしたことからプロテニスの試合では黄色いボールが使われているのです。

Why are left-handed pitchers called a "southpaw"?

The word "southpaw" comes from early baseball history. Traditionally, baseball diamonds were built so that home plate was in the west. This was so that batters would not have to look directly into the afternoon sun. This meant that the pitcher would face west, with his right arm to the north and his left arm to the south.

When a pitcher was left-handed, he was called a "southpaw" because the "paw," or hand, that he used would be in the south.

Sports スポーツ

なぜ左利きのピッチャーは「サウスポー」と呼ばれるの？

　「サウスポー」という言葉は野球の歴史の黎明期に始まっています。伝統的に野球場のダイヤモンドはホームベースが西になるように作られています。そうすることでバッターが午後の太陽光線を直接見なくてすむからです。したがってピッチャーは西に顔を向けることになり、右腕が北、左腕が南に向くことになります。

　でもピッチャーが左利きの場合、「ポー」(訳注：pawは通常「動物の爪のある足」のことを意味する単語ですが、人の手もそれになぞらえているわけです)、つまり利き手が南向きになることから、「サウスポー」と呼ばれたわけです。

Why are races always run counterclockwise?

First of all, it's important to note that not all races are run counterclockwise. In England, for example, many horseraces go clockwise. It's the same for Australia's NASCAR. But in general, most races—whether it's the 200-meter men's race in the Olympics or the Indianapolis 500—are run counterclockwise. Why is this?

Nobody knows for sure, but there are a few theories. One is that because most humans are right-handed, the natural movement of the human body when making a circle is to go towards the left.

Sports スポーツ

どうして競走では時計の反対回りに走るの？

　まず第一に、必ずしもすべてのレースが反時計回りに走るわけではないことは断っておく必要があります。たとえばイギリスでは多くの競馬が時計回りにまわりますし、オーストラリアのNASCARも同様です。そうは言ってもオリンピックの男子200メートル走もインディアナポリス500もそうですが、ほとんどの競技が反時計回りに走るのは確かです。ではそれはなぜなのでしょう？

　確定的なことは誰にも言えないのですが、いくつかの説があります。そのひとつは、ほとんどの人は右利きで、円を描くとき人の体の自然な動きは左回りになるからというものです。

Another theory has to do just with horseraces in America. Back in 1780, the man who built the first circular horserace track in America, William Whitley, was a big supporter of the American Revolution. So he built his race track going counterclockwise, just to be different from England, which built their race tracks going clockwise.

As for car racing in America, races are run counterclockwise because drivers sit on the left-hand side of the car, and going counterclockwise allows them to see the turns much better.

However, nobody has a very good explanation about why most races around the world go in this direction.

Sports スポーツ

　もうひとつの説はアメリカにおける競馬と関係があります。1780年にアメリカで最初の円形の競馬場を作ったウィリアム・ホイットリー氏が、熱心なアメリカ革命支持者だったため、レーストラックを時計回りに回るイギリスとは反対の反時計回りにしたのだ、というものです。

　アメリカのカーレースがそうですが、レースではドライバーが車の左側に座るため、反時計回りの方がターンする方向を見やすいこともあり、反時計回りに走ることになっているのです。

　いずれにしても、ほとんどのレースがその方向に向かって走行する理由として完全に満足のいく説明ができる人はいないのです。

The Human Body
人のからだ

Why do people float in water?

Most people can float in water because their bodies are not as dense as the water. Density is how tightly packed physical matter is. So, for example, lead is denser than a piece of wood, because the molecules that make up lead are packed much more tightly together than the molecules that make up wood.

For the most part, human bodies are less dense than water, and that's why they can float. However, muscles are more dense than fat. So, people with a lot of fat will have an easier time floating than people without much fat.

The Human Body 人のからだ

どうして人は水の中で浮くの？

　ほとんどの人は、身体が水ほどの密度を持っていないため水の中では浮くのです。「密度」とは何かと言うと、物質がどれだけ密に詰め込まれているかということです。したがって、たとえば鉛は木よりも密度が高いと言うことができます。これは鉛を成り立たせている分子が、木を成り立たせている分子よりもギュウギュウに詰め込まれているからです。

　ほとんどの部分で、人の体は水ほどの密度を持っていないので浮くことができます。ところで筋肉は脂肪よりも密度が高いのです。ですから、脂肪のあまりない人よりも脂肪をたくさん蓄えている人の方が、簡単に水に浮くことができるのです。

How many bones are in a human body?

Human babies are born with anywhere between 300 to 350 bones, but as they become adults, the number changes to 206. As a human child grows up, some of their bones—such as parts of the skull or bones in the hips—grow together to become one larger bone.

Of the 206 bones in an adult human body, 106 of them are in the hands and feet. That's more than half of all human bones!

The Human Body 人のからだ

人の体にはいくつの骨があるの？

　人が生まれたときの体の骨数は、だいたい300〜350の間であるとされていますが、成人するとその数は206本になっています。人の子どもが成長するにしたがって、頭蓋骨やお尻の骨なども成長していきひとつの大きな骨に変わるのです。

　おとなの体の206本の骨のうち、106本もの骨が手や足に集中しています。実に骨の半分以上は手や足の骨だということになります。

How much human hair grows in a day?

Although it depends on the person, the human hair grows about 0.4 millimeters in one day. That means hair grows about 1.25 centimeters per month, and 15 centimeters per year.

However, how fast hair will grow can sometimes change depending on health, nutrition, and age.

人の髪の毛は
1日にどれだけ伸びるの？

　人によって違いはあるものの、髪の毛は1日で0.4mmほど伸びます。ということは、ひと月では1.25cm、1年では15cmほど伸びることになります。

　でも時として髪の伸びは健康や栄養状態、そして年齢によって左右されることもあるでしょう。

Why do people's teeth chatter when they are scared?

Teeth chattering is a natural physical reaction to fear that the human body is programmed to do. Early on in the history of human evolution, humans used their teeth to protect themselves. When faced with a great threat, the human body instantly got ready to either attack or run away.

To attack, the mouth muscles would tighten so that the teeth were ready to bite. To run away, the leg muscles would tighten so that the legs were ready to move. The tightened mouth muscles make the teeth chatter, and the tightened leg muscles make the legs feel wobbly.

Although people today no longer have to protect themselves with their teeth, the human body still reacts to fear with the tightening of these muscles.

The Human Body 人のからだ

どうして人は怖い目にあうと歯がガチガチいうの？

　歯がガチガチいうのは恐怖に対する身体の自然な反応で、そのようになるように体が作られているのです。人の進化の過程で初期の頃、人は自らを守るために歯を使ったのです。深刻な危機に出合ったとき、人の体は直ちに敵と戦うか逃げるかを判断しなければなりませんでした。

　戦うとしたら口の筋肉は引き締まり、歯は相手をいつでも噛みつけるようになります。逃げるとしたら足の筋肉が引き締まり、いつでも動けるようになります。口の筋肉が緊張すると、歯はガチガチいうようになり、足の筋肉が緊張すると、足がグラグラしたりします。

　人類は今では自分たちを歯で護身することはなくなりましたが、体はまだ恐怖に対してこうした筋肉を引き締めようと反応するのです。

Why does eating spicy foods make some people sweat?

Have you ever felt your face get hot and maybe even start to sweat when you eat a hot pepper? That's because your brain actually thinks your body temperature is rising.

Spicy foods have a chemical that sends a signal to the nerves in your mouth that is the same signal as a rise in temperature. The nerves tell your brain that your body is becoming hot, and your brain tells your body to start sweating to cool you down.

The Human Body 人のからだ

辛い食べ物を食べるとどうして汗をかくの？

　唐辛子を食べると顔が火照ったり、場合によっては汗をかいたりすることはありませんか？　どうしてそうなるかというと、脳はあなたの体温が上がり始めていると判断しているからです。

　実は辛い食べ物には口の中の神経に体温上昇の時と同じ信号を送る化学物質が含まれているのです。この神経が脳に向かって「体の温度が上がっているよ」と告げるので、今度は脳が体に向かって汗をかいて体温を下げるような命令を下すのです。

Why do humans have body hair?

There are different reasons for why we have hair on different parts of our bodies. Scientists say that early humans had much more body hair, similar to that of chimpanzees or apes. But humans slowly lost this hair during evolution because much of the hair became unnecessary.

Scientists think that the hair we did keep, such as on our heads and under our arms, all serve a purpose.

The hair on our heads protects our heads from the sun. But hair in the underarm and genital areas may serve a purpose in sexual selection.

These areas of the body hold glands that give off scents that are different for every person. These scents are thought to attract members of the opposite sex, similar to the way pheromones work in animals. The hair in those areas helps to trap the smells and makes them more noticeable.

The Human Body 人のからだ

人にはどうして毛が生えているの？

　体の部位によって毛が生えている理由は異なります。科学者によれば黎明期の人類にはチンパンジーや類人猿のように体毛がもっと生えていたそうです。ところが、これほどの毛が必要でなくなったため進化の過程でゆっくりと毛を失っていったのです。

　髪の毛やわき毛など現在生えている体毛には、すべてなんらかの目的があるというのが科学者の見解です。

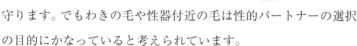

　頭の毛は太陽光線から頭を守ります。でもわきの毛や性器付近の毛は性的パートナーの選択の目的にかなっていると考えられています。

　このエリアには人によって異なる匂いを出す分泌腺があります。こうした匂いは動物の世界におけるフェロモンと似たはたらきで、異性を惹きつけるものと考えられています。そしてこうした場所の体毛は匂いをとらえて、より異性に気づかれやすくするはたらきがあるというわけです。

Why do fingers and toes wrinkle in water?

Water washes away a natural body oil called sebum. When sebum is washed away, dead skin cells absorb the water and swell up.

However, there is a layer of living skin cells under the dead skin, which does not absorb the water and stays the same. The swelling cells are connected to this deeper layer, so the connections between the swelling cells and the normal cells make the outer layer of skin look wrinkly.

The reason why only fingertips and toes get these wrinkles is because these areas have more layers of both the living and dead skin cells than any other part of the body.

The Human Body 人のからだ

手や足の指は水に浸けると どうしてしわができるの？

　水は皮脂と呼ばれる体の天然の油分を洗い流してしまいます。皮脂が洗い流されると死んだ皮膚の細胞が水を吸って膨れます。

　ところが死んだ皮膚の下には生きた皮膚細胞の層があって、それは水を吸収しないためそのまま維持されます。膨れた細胞はより深い層とつながっているので、膨れ上がった細胞と正常な細胞がつながることによって皮膚の外側の層がしわに見えるのです。

　指先やつま先だけにこうしたしわができる理由は、こうした場所は生きた細胞と死んだ細胞の層の数がほかの体の部位よりも多いためです。

Why do humans dream?

There is still no "correct" answer to why humans dream, and scientists continue to study dreaming to see if there is a purpose to it. There are a few common theories as to why we dream.

One theory holds that dreaming is a way for the brain to process and understand all the information it collects during the day. Another theory is that dreams are a way for the brain to work out human emotions. During the day, the brain is hard at work solving problems, learning things, and telling the body how to move and what to do. Some say that dreaming is a time for the brain to focus just on emotions.

One last theory is that dreaming has no real purpose at all, but is simply a product of the brain's scattered thoughts while it has no specific job at hand.

どうして人は夢を見るの？

いまだにどうして人が夢を見るのかという問いに対して、これという絶対に正しい答えは見つけ出されていませんが、どんな目的があるのかを知るために夢の研究は続けられています。どうして夢を見るかに関しては有名ないくつかの仮説があります。

ひとつの説によれば、夢を見るのは日中に集めたさまざまな情報を脳が処理し理解するための方法なのだということです。別の説は、人の感情を脳がうまくおさめるための方法になっているというものです。日中、脳は問題を解決したり学習したり、体に動きやすべきことを指令するなど酷使されています。つまり夢とは脳が感情の動きだけに集中するための時間なのだというわけです。

最後の説としては夢はとりわけ何の目的も持っていないというもので、脳が何もやるべき仕事を持っていないときに頭の中で散り散りになった考えが作り出すだけのものだ、というものです。

Why do humans laugh?

There are many possible reasons as to why humans laugh. First of all, many researchers believe that laughter is a natural way to make human relationships stronger. People laugh with each other when they feel comfortable with each other, and the more they laugh together, the more comfortable they get.

Another theory is that laughter began as a way to share a sense of relief from surviving something dangerous together. This could have led to laughter being a way for humans to show trust for each another.

Finally, laughter could also be a way to control the actions of a group. Laughter is very much a social activity—when a person in control laughs, such as a teacher or a boss, almost everybody else in the room laughs along. So some researchers believe that laughter evolved as a way of showing power over a group.

どうして人は笑うの？

　人が笑うのにはたくさんのもっともらしい理由があります。まず第一に、多くの研究者が笑いは人間関係を強固にするための自然な方法のひとつであると説明しています。人々は互いに心地よいと感じると笑いを共有し、笑えば笑うほど打ち解け合うものです。

　また笑いは、危機的状況から解放されたときの安堵感を共有する方法として生まれたとする説もあります。相互に信頼していることを見せ合う方法として笑いが機能したということです。

　最後に、笑いは集団の行動をコントロールする機能を持つという説があります。言い換えると、笑いは社会的行為そのものだということです。たとえば、教師やリーダーのような指導的立場の人が笑うと、同じ部屋にいるほとんど誰もが笑うというようなことです。つまりある研究によれば、笑いは集団に力を示すための方法として発展したということになります。

Why do people cry?

There are three types of human tears: one is for protecting the eye and keeping it wet, another is for cleaning the eye when something foreign enters it, and the third is a way to release emotion.

When people feel sadness or pain, their bodies often produce tears. These "emotion" tears hold a higher amount of two chemicals, manganese and prolactin. Scientists say that crying out these two chemicals through tears balances the body's chemical levels and eases tension in the body, making the person feel better.

Other researchers say that crying is also a powerful form of communication. As babies, crying is the first way that humans learn to express themselves, and as adults, crying continues to tell other people how we feel. Whether it is a form of creating chemical balance within the body or expressing our feelings to others, crying is natural part of being human.

The Human Body 人のからだ

どうして人は泣くの？

　人の涙には3つのタイプがあります。ひとつは目を湿らせて守るというもの。ふたつ目は何か異物が入ったときに洗い流す機能。そして3つめは感情を解放する機能です。

　人は悲しみや苦痛を感じると、身体が涙を作り出します。この感情的涙はマンガンとプロラクチン（黄体刺激ホルモン）という2種類の化学物質を多く含んでいます。ある研究によれば、泣くことでこの2種類の化学物質を涙のかたちで排泄し、身体の化学物質の量のバランスを変え、体の緊張をほぐし、気分をよくするということです。

　泣くことの別の側面として、非常に力を持ったコミュニケーションのひとつだというものがあります。赤ん坊がそうであるように、泣くことは人が自己をどう表現するかを学習する最初の方法と言えますし、おとなにとっても泣くことは他の人々にどのように感じているのかを伝える方法として機能し続けている面があります。体の中の化学物質のバランスを取るためであるにせよ、他者に対する感情の発露であるにせよ、泣くことは人が人であることの一部と言えるでしょう。

Why does hair turn gray?

As people grow older, they stop producing a chemical called melanin, which produces hair color. The more melanin a person has, the darker their hair is, and the less melanin they have, the lighter their hair color.

When hair grows without melanin, the hair cells are left without color, turning it white or gray.

The Human Body 人のからだ

どうして白髪が生えてくるの？

　人は成長するにつれ、メラニン（色素）と呼ばれる化学物質を作るのを止めてしまいます。これは髪の色になる物質です。髪の毛の色は、メラニンをたくさん持っている人ほど濃くなり、少ない人ほど明るい色になります。

　髪がメラニン色素なしに成長してしまうと、髪の毛の細胞には色がないので、結果として白髪やグレイヘアーになるわけです。

Why are some people right-handed and some people left-handed?

Although there is no single answer for this question, it is generally agreed that it has to do with the way the human brain works. The brain has two sides that work together to control different human actions. The left side of the brain controls the right side of the body, while the right side of the brain controls the left side of the body.

Many studies have found that most people control speech and language—including writing—with the left side of their brain, so this leads to a high number of people who prefer to use their right hands to write.

In addition to this, scientists have recently found that genes seem to also determine which hand a person will use as their main hand. The gene known as LRRTM1 can develop in two ways: it can either be a D gene or a C gene.

The Human Body 人のからだ

どうして右利きや左利きの違いが起きるの？

　この問いに対してはひとつの確定的な答えがあるわけではないのですが、一般的に人の脳のはたらきに関連があるという点に関しては見解が一致しています。脳は2つに分かれていて、さまざまな人の活動をコントロールするために協力し合っているのです。左脳は体の右側を制御し、右脳は体の左側を制御しています。

　さまざまな研究によって、ほとんどの人は発話と言語（書くことも含む）のコントロールを左脳を使って行っているため、大多数の人々が右手で書くことを好むと言われています。

　これに加え、最近の研究では利き手がどちらになるのかは遺伝子がどうも関係しているようだということもわかってきています。LRRTM1と呼ばれる遺伝子はD遺伝子とC遺伝子のどちらかに発展することができます。

People with the D type of gene are usually right-handed. People with the C type of gene are not always left-handed, but the C gene seems to introduce an element of chance: 50 percent of people with the C gene are right-handed, while the other 50 percent are left-handed.

In future studies, scientists hope to know more about how this gene and the brain work together to determine how the body functions.

The Human Body 人のからだ

　Ｄタイプの遺伝子をもった人々は通常右利きになります。Ｃタイプの遺伝子をもった人々は必ずしも左利きにはなりませんが、そうなる潜在的要素が高いと思われています。具体的にはＣ遺伝子をもった人々の50％が右利きになり、残りの50％が左利きになるそうです。

　将来、研究によってこの遺伝子と脳がどのように関与しあいながら体の機能に影響を与えるのかがわかってくるのではないか、と科学者たちは予想しています。

Why do people catch more colds in the winter?

There is actually no evidence that cold weather causes people to catch more colds. Germs cause colds and sickness, not the winter. However, there are more cases of influenza during the winter months.

This could be because more people stay inside because it's cold outside and shut their windows and doors, trapping themselves in with germs.

Others say it's because people feel more stress during the cold months. Sometimes signs of stress can be a runny nose, a headache, and other minor aches and pains that seem similar to catching a cold.

But there is actually no proof that cold temperatures make people sick.

The Human Body 人のからだ

どうして冬になると風邪をひきやすくなるの？

　実は、寒い気候になると風邪をひきやすくなるという確たる証拠はないのです。細菌が風邪やその他の病気の原因であって、冬が原因ではないのです。でも冬の数ヵ月にインフルエンザにかかるケースが多いのは事実です。

　これは外が寒い時期、人は屋内にいることが多くなって窓や戸を閉めきるために、細菌を自分たちと一緒に部屋の中に閉じ込めてしまうということが考えられています。

　また、寒い冬の季節に人はよりストレスを感じるからだと考える向きもあります。時々、こうした症状として鼻水や頭痛、そして体の他の部位の痛みなど、まるで風邪をひいたのと似たようなストレスを訴える場合があります。

　いずれにしても、寒い季節が風邪をひきやすくするという明確な証拠というものは存在しないのです。

Why do we itch?

When we feel an itch on our bodies, it is our brain's way of telling us that there is something irritating the body. It's a way to protect the body from things that can be small but harmful, such as bugs.

When we feel an itch, we react by scratching, which is a way to brush aside whatever is on the body.

The Human Body 人のからだ

どうしてかゆいと感じるの？

　わたしたちが体にかゆみを覚えるとき、それは体のどこかにいらだたせるものがあるということを脳が教えているのです。これはまた小さいながらも何か害を及ぼすようなもの、たとえば、小さな虫などから体を守るための方法なのです。

　どこかにかゆみがあるとき、私たちはそれに掻くことで反応します。それは体の表面にある何かを払いのけようとしているのです。

Why does yawning make other people yawn?

Have you ever noticed that when you see someone yawn, all of a sudden you feel like yawning too? Scientists say that yawning together can be a way for a group to feel connected and close. But while many animals yawn, group yawning only applies to humans, chimpanzees, and, some say, dogs.

It is similar to how groups will often start laughing when one person laughs, or how people will start to cry if someone else is crying. However, scientists have not yet figured out exactly why people and animals yawn.

The Human Body 人のからだ

どうしてあくびは他人に伝染するの？

　誰かがあくびをしたら、突然自分もあくびしたくなったことはありませんか？　科学者によれば、あくびを一緒にするのは集団が連結感や親近感を感じるためである可能性があるようです。でも多くの動物があくびをする一方で、集団であくびをするのは、人、チンパンジー、そして（なんと）犬だけだと言います。

　これは、ひとりの人が笑ったり泣いたりするのにつられてどれだけよく集団が一緒に笑い始めたり泣き始めたりするのか、ということにも似ています。それでもなお、研究者たちはどうして人や動物があくびをするのかという理由を正確には解明していないのです。

Why do our voices sound so different on recordings?

Lots of times when we hear our own voice on a recording, we are totally surprised. "That's not what I sound like!" we say to ourselves. The voice we hear on the recording usually sounds higher than we think we sound.

So what do we actually sound like? Is the recording correct, or is the voice we hear in our heads when we talk correct? And why are the two voices so different?

The voice on the recording is what we actually sound like to everybody else. The reason why our own voice sounds so different to us is because we are hearing our voice with our inner ear as well as our outer ear. What does that mean, exactly?

The Human Body 人のからだ

どうして声は録音すると違って聞こえるの？

　私たちは自分の声が録音されたのを聞くと、まったく驚いてしまうことがよくあります。誰もが「自分の声はこんなじゃない」と言うのです。録音された声は、自分が聞いているのよりも高い声として聞こえます。

　実際問題、自分の声というのはどう聞こえているのでしょう？録音が正しいのでしょうか。それとも話しているときに自分の頭に響いてくる声が正しいのでしょうか。それにしてもどうしてふたつの声にはこのような違いが生じるのでしょう？

　録音された声は、実際に自分以外のみんなが聞いている声です。自分が聞いている声とこれほどに違うのは、私たちは自分の声を内側からと外側から同時に聞いているからです。でもそれってどういう意味なのでしょう？

When we talk, the sounds we make travel through the bones in our neck and head and are picked up by our inner ear. At the same time, our outer ear picks up the sound of our voice coming out of our mouth and traveling through the air. A mixture of these two sounds is what we hear when we hear ourselves talk.

But what everybody else hears, and of course what is recorded, is just the sound of our voice traveling through the air.

The Human Body 人のからだ

　私たちが話をするとき、その音は首や頭の骨を通って、体の内側の耳によって拾われます。同時に、口から発声されて空気を通って運ばれてくる音声も外側の耳によって拾われます。これら2種類の音のミックスされたものが、私たちが話をするときに自分自身に聞こえている声なのです。

　一方、他の人たちが聞いている声、そしてもちろん録音された声は、空気だけを経由してきた音なのです。

Is reading in the dark really bad for your eyes?

Although our parents may have told us all our lives that reading in the dark is bad for our eyes, there is no hard evidence that shows it will damage our vision. Most doctors say that your family history is what influences the health of your eyes. Also, old age can be a big reason for the weakening of vision.

However, many doctors agree that working your eyes too hard as a child may make you more likely to have weak vision later in life.

The Human Body 人のからだ

暗いところで字を読むと目が悪くなるの？

　「暗いところで読むと目が悪くなりますよ」と、ご両親はいつも口癖のように言ってきたかもしれませんが、実はそれが私たちの視力を悪くするということには確たる裏付けがないのです。ほとんどの医者はあなたの目の健康に影響を与えるのは遺伝だと言うでしょう。あとは加齢が視力の衰えの有力な原因である可能性があります。

　でも、多くの医者は、幼少期に目を酷使すると、後年に視力を落とす可能性が高いということには賛同しています。

Why do we sometimes wake up sweating when we have a bad dream?

When we have a bad dream, our bodies go through stress just like when we are awake. Feeling anxiety or feeling afraid, even when asleep, can make the heart beat faster and raise the body's blood pressure. This causes sweating.

The Human Body 人のからだ

こわい夢を見て目が覚めると なぜ汗をかいていたりするの？

　悪い夢を見ると、私たちの体は私たちが起きているときのようなストレスを経験します。不安や恐怖を感じると、もし寝ていたとしても、私たちの心臓の鼓動は早くなりますし、血圧も上がってしまいます。こうした反応が汗をかく原因となるのです。

Nature and Animals
自然と動物

What is the temperature of the sun?

The sun, which is the largest object in the solar system, is about 93 million miles from Earth. But its light and heat are so powerful that it makes life on Earth possible. So how hot is the sun, really?

The sun exists in layers, with the highest temperatures in the sun's core—the part that is furthest inside. The sun's core can burn as hot as 15 million degrees Celsius. The temperature is so high here because this is where nuclear fusion happens. From here, energy and heat moves out to a layer called the convective zone. Here, the temperature reaches about 2 million degrees Celsius.

The next layer out is the photosphere, which reaches about 5,500 degrees Celsius. It is here that the heat and energy of the sun becomes what we know as light.

Nature and Animals 自然と動物

太陽の温度は何度なの？

　太陽系の中で最大の物体である太陽は、地球からおよそ9300万マイル（約1億5000万km）離れています。でもその光と熱は地球に生命を育むほどのパワーを持っています。では、太陽はいったいどれくらいの熱さなのでしょうか？

　太陽は層状になっていて、最も高い温度は表面から一番深いところにある核の部分です。太陽の核は摂氏1500万度であると考えられています。温度がこれほどに高いのはそこで核融合が起きているからです。ここからエネルギーと熱が「対流層」と呼ばれる場所に向かって移動します。そこでは摂氏200万度くらいになっています。

　次の外層は「光球」と呼ばれ、摂氏5500度くらいになっています。太陽の熱やエネルギーが私たちに見えている太陽光になる場所です。

After the photosphere, the energy and light moves into the chromosphere, which is the coolest part of the sun. Temperatures here only rise to about 4,320 degrees Celsius. Then, as heat moves to the last layer, the corona, the temperatures rise again, sometimes burning as hot as 2 million degrees Celsius. After the energy is burned up here, the sun's matter is blown away into space.

Nature and Animals 自然と動物

　光球を過ぎると、エネルギーと光は太陽で最も温度の低い「彩層」に移動します。ここの温度はおよそ摂氏4320度にまでしか上がりません。そして熱は最表層の「コロナ（光冠）」と呼ばれるところに到達し、そこで温度は再び上昇し、摂氏200万度くらいで燃焼します。エネルギーはここで燃え尽き、太陽の物質は宇宙空間に吹き出されるのです。

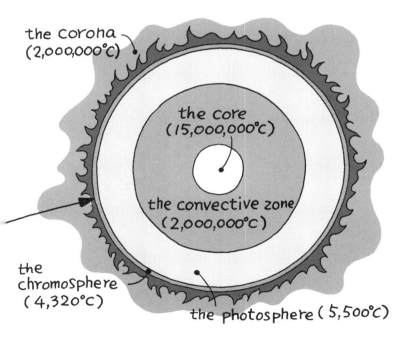

Why are there 365 days in a year?

A year is the time it takes for the Earth to go once around the sun, which is actually 365.25 days. When ancient peoples made the calendar, it was difficult to mark a space for .25 days, so they decided to create an extra day every four years, when the four instances of .25 days would add up to one whole day. This is why we have a leap year every four years.

Nature and Animals 自然と動物

どうして1年は365日なの？

　地球が太陽のまわりを1周するのにかかるのが1年で、それは実際には365.25日です。大昔の人々がカレンダーを作ったとき、0.25日という余白を表示するのは難しかったので、0.25に4を掛けると1日になる計算により、4年に一度特別な日を設けることにしたのです。これが4年に一度 閏 年が来る理由なのです。

Why does smoke come from fire?

Some fires seem to have more smoke than others. Why is this? What is smoke, and why does it come from fire?

Smoke is what is given off when chemicals start to burn. For example, if you add a new piece of wood to a burning fire, the wood will give off smoke before it starts to really burn. This is because there are a number of chemicals and other elements, such as water, in the wood. These chemicals burn at different rates, and when they burn, they give off carbon, which is carried on the air as smoke. However, once the chemicals have all been turned to carbon, the smoke disappears.

Nature and Animals 自然と動物

なぜ煙は火のあるところから出てくるの？

　ある種の火は特に煙をよく出すということがありますが、それはなぜでしょう？　そもそも煙とは何なのでしょうか？　そしてそれはどうして火から出てくるのでしょうか？

　煙とは化学物質が燃焼するときに放出されるものです。たとえば、燃えている火の中に新しい木をくべると、木は本格的に燃え始める前に煙を出します。これは木の中に何種類もの化学物質や水などの雑多な成分が含まれているためです。これらの化学物質は異なる比率で燃え、それらは燃えるとき炭素を放出したりします。それは煙として空気によって運び出されるのです。しかし、化学物質がすべて炭素に変わってしまうと、煙は出なくなるのです。

Why is seawater salty?

Seawater isn't just water—it contains 50 quadrillion (or 50 million billion) tons of mineral salts and solid matter in the water. These salts mostly come from the earth's outer layer. As rains wash away dirt and rocks from the earth into rivers, the rivers carry these solids into the ocean. The ocean also contains an incredible amount of dead plant and animal matter, so it can be said that ocean water has a little bit of everything in it.

Nature and Animals 自然と動物

どうして海の水は塩辛いの？

　海水は単なる水ではありません。それは5京（10億の5000万倍）トンの無機塩と固形物質を水の中に含んでいます。こうした塩はほとんどが地球の地表から来たものです。雨が土や岩石を地表から川へと洗い流し、川がこうした固形物を海の中に運び込むのです。海は途方もない量の死んだ植物や動物といった物質を含んでいるので、海の水はそうしたかつて生き物だったものが含んでいたあらゆるものを少しずつ保持しているのです。

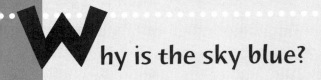
Why is the sky blue?

During the day, the sky is blue because the molecules that are in the air scatter blue and purple light from the sun more than any other color. The light from the sun, which looks white, is actually a mix of all the seven colors of the rainbow: red, orange, yellow, green, blue, indigo, and purple.

But when the light from the sun hits the molecules in the air, blue and purple are scattered the most. Since the human eye can't see purple light that well, what we see in the sky is mostly blue.

Nature and Animals 自然と動物

どうして空は青いの？

　日中空が青く見えるのは、大気中に含まれる分子が太陽からの青や紫色の光を他の色よりも多く散乱させているからです。白く見える太陽からの光は、実際は虹の7色、つまり赤、オレンジ、黄、緑、青、藍、そして紫のすべてを混ぜたものです。

　ところが、太陽光が大気中の分子に当たると、青と紫だけが一番分散されます。人の目は紫色の光をよくとらえることができないため、私たちの目には空の色はほぼ青い色として見えるのです。

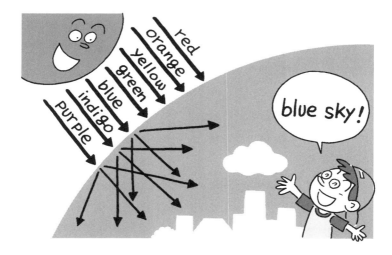

Why are clouds white?

The reason that clouds look white is similar to the reason why the sky is blue. Clouds are formed by tiny drops of water and ice that hang together in the air. These drops scatter all the colors from the sun equally: red, orange, yellow, green, blue, indigo, and purple.

When all these colors are scattered together, the human eye sees no color at all—in other words, white.

Nature and Animals 自然と動物

なぜ雲は白いの？

　雲が白く見える理由は空が青く見える理由に近いものがあります。雲は水や氷の細かな粒が集まって大気中で留まっているものです。この小さな粒は太陽からもたらされる色（赤、オレンジ、黄、緑、青、藍、そして紫）のすべてをまき散らしています。

　こうした色がいっせいに散乱すると、人の目には色がないように見えるのです。つまり白に見えるということです。

Why do stars sometimes look like they are blinking?

When seen from Earth, it often looks like stars are blinking and changing colors. But they are not actually blinking. It only appears that way because there are many dust and gas molecules in the air surrounding Earth.

When light from the stars passes through these particles, sometimes the appearance of the star's brightness and color can change.

Nature and Animals 自然と動物

なぜ星は瞬いているように見えることがあるの？

　地球から見ると、星々はしばしば瞬いているように見えたり色を変えているように見えたりします。でも実際は瞬いているわけではありません。地球を取り囲んでいる大気中の塵やガスの分子があるせいで、私たちの目にそのように見えているだけなのです。

　星からの光がこうした粒子を通ってくると、星の明るさや色が変わって見えることがあるのです。

Why do tree leaves turn color in autumn?

Plants make food by turning light from the sun and water into sugar. A special plant chemical called chlorophyll helps plants make this happen, and chlorophyll is what gives plants their green color.

As summer turns into autumn, the days get shorter, and there is less and less light for the plant to make sugar. So, plants know it's time to rest. They stop trying to create sugar with water and light and instead live off of the sugar they have stored.

As the plants begin to rest, they stop producing chlorophyll, making leaves lose their green color. Some leaves start turning yellow and orange, which were colors that always existed in the leaves but were covered up by the chlorophyll.

Some leaves turn bright red or purple because the light from the sun turns the sugars trapped in the leaves into a red or purple color. Some leaves turn brown because there is waste matter left in the leaves.

Nature and Animals 自然と動物

どうして木の葉は秋になると色が変わるの？

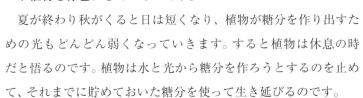

植物は太陽からの光と水を糖に換えることで自分の栄養にしています。植物だけに固有のクロロフィルと呼ばれる化学物質がこれを可能にしており、このクロロフィルが植物を緑色にしているのです。

夏が終わり秋がくると日は短くなり、植物が糖分を作り出すための光もどんどん弱くなっていきます。すると植物は休息の時だと悟るのです。植物は水と光から糖分を作ろうとするのを止めて、それまでに貯めておいた糖分を使って生き延びるのです。

植物が休みに入ると、クロロフィルを製造するのも止めてしまうので、葉の緑色は失われるのです。葉によっては、クロロフィルによって覆われていた元々葉が持っている色が見えてきて、黄色くなったりオレンジ色になったりするのです。

葉の中には明るい赤や紫色になるものもあります。それは太陽からの光が葉の中に閉じ込められていた糖分に作用するためです。茶色くなる葉もありますが、それは葉の中に残っている老廃物のためです。

Why can you hear the ocean when you hold a seashell to your ear?

When you hold a seashell up to your ear, you can hear a quiet roar that sounds like the waves of the ocean. But this sound is actually the noise all around you. The seashell captures all the noises that surround you and echoes them quietly within the shell. The size and shape of the shell, as well as the loudness of the noises that surround you, affect the sound you will hear.

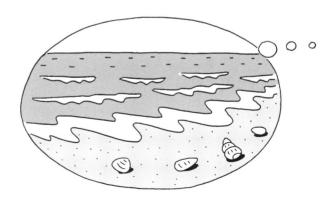

Nature and Animals 自然と動物

なぜ巻貝を耳に当てると海の音が聞こえるの？

　貝殻を耳に当てると、海の波のような静かに鳴る「ゴーッ」というような音を聞くことができます。でもこの音は実は自分の周りにある雑音なのです。巻貝は周りに存在するさまざまな雑音を捕らえて、貝殻の中でそれを静かにこだまさせます。貝殻の大きさや形や、周囲の雑音の音量などにもよって、聞こえる音は左右されます。

Does the color red really anger bulls?

For centuries, bull fighters (or matadors) have used red capes to make bulls charge at them. But the truth is, the color red doesn't really upset bulls at all. Bulls are actually red-green color-blind and can't see the color red.

What does bother the bull is the waving movement of the cape. The only reason that bull fighters use red capes is that it hides blood stains and has become a bull fighting tradition.

Nature and Animals 自然と動物

赤色は本当に牛を怒らせるの？

　何世紀もの間、闘牛士（マタドール）たちは雄牛をけしかけるのに赤いケープを使ってきました。ところが真相はどうかというと、赤い色が雄牛を怒らせることは全くないのです。雄牛は赤と緑を区別できない色盲であり、赤を認識できないのです。

　雄牛をいらだたせるのはケープのひらひらする動きです。闘牛士たちが赤いケープを使うのは血の染みを目立たせないためで、それが闘牛の伝統となっているのです。

Why do bats sleep upside down?

Bats are nocturnal animals, meaning they are active during the night and sleep during the day. But because the day is so bright, bats had to find dark places to sleep, such as caves. But they could not sleep on the floor of a cave because they could easily be found and eaten by bigger cave animals, such as wolves.

Instead, they naturally evolved a way to sleep on the ceiling of the cave, where wolves and other animals could not get to them. Over time, the bat came to be able to sleep while hanging upside down from the ceiling of caves.

Nature and Animals 自然と動物

なぜコウモリは逆さになって眠るの？

　コウモリは夜行性の動物なので、夜に活動し日中は眠っているのです。でも日中はとても明るいため、コウモリは洞窟のような暗い場所を寝場所として探さなければなりません。ところが洞窟の床で眠っているわけにはいきません。オオカミなどの、より大型の洞窟にいる動物に容易に見つかって食べられてしまうからです。

　そこで必然的に、コウモリはオオカミなどの動物に簡単に捕まってしまわない場所として、洞窟の天井で眠るように進化したのです。時とともにコウモリは洞窟の天井から逆さまにぶら下がりながら眠ることができるようになっていったのです。

Do fish ever sleep?

Because fish never close their eyes, it looks like they're always awake. But fish do get their sleep.

When fish need to rest, they often move to areas with calm, still waters. They stop moving and their bodies go into a deep rest period. They do not close their eyes, but their bodies stop working in much the same way that humans stop unnecessary actions during sleep.

Nature and Animals 自然と動物

魚は眠ることがあるの？

　魚は目を閉じることがないため、いつでも起きているように見えます。でも魚も眠るのです。

　魚は休みたいと感じると、静かで水の動きのない場所に移動します。動きは止まり、体は深い休息に入ります。目は閉じませんが、体の機能が停止するという現象は、人が睡眠中不必要な活動を停めることと同じです。

Why do cats purr?

Researchers say there may be several reasons why cats purr, but they all agree on how it happens: the cat's brain sends messages to the throat muscles, making them shake at a rate between 25 to 150 vibrations per second. Then, when the cat takes a breath in or out, the sound of purring is produced.

Some scientists say that purring is a form of communication. It can signal to others that the cat is happy, hungry, or even frightened. But other scientists think purring might help healing processes in the cat's body.

One researcher, Elizabeth von Muggenthaler, says that vibrations of 24 to 140 per second produce a healing effect for bone growth and repair. She believes that certain cats may have evolved the purr as a way to help heal their wounds.

Nature and Animals 自然と動物

どうして猫は
ゴロゴロ言うの？

　なぜ猫が喉をゴロゴロ言わせるのかに関してはいくつかの理由があるとされていますが、どのようにそれが起こるのかについての説明は一致しています。つまり猫の脳が喉の筋肉に命令を送り、1秒間に25〜150回くらいの振動を起こさせるのです。そのときに猫が呼吸して呼気が出たり入ったりすると、その音が発生するのです。

　科学者の中にはゴロゴロという音はコミュニケーションの一種だと主張する人もいます。猫が嬉しかったり、空腹だったり、場合によっては何かに怖がったりしたときに他の猫にそれを伝えるためのシグナルかもしれないということです。また、この音は猫自身の身体の癒しのプロセスである可能性を指摘する研究者もいます。

　その一人、エリザベス・フォン・ムッゲンテーラーは1秒間に24〜140回の振動は骨の成長や（傷を）治したりするヒーリング効果があると言っています。彼女によれば猫は怪我をしたとき、怪我から回復させる方法としてゴロゴロという音を出すように進化したのだと言うのです。

Why do horses have to wear "shoes"?

Horses have existed for a long time in the wild without having to wear metal shoes on their hooves. So why do people make their horses wear shoes?

The answer has to do with how humans have taken horses out of the wild. In the wild, horses run free and are always moving—some horses will even move twenty miles a day to find a new source of food. Because of this frequent movement, wild horses grow good, strong hooves on their own. The old hoof gets worn down naturally and is replaced with the new growth.

However, when humans took horses out of the wild, they raised them to live according to human lifestyles. Horses stopped running free and spent long parts of the day standing still in an animal pen. Some even had to get used to walking or running on paved roads.

Nature and Animals 自然と動物

馬はどうして「靴」（蹄鉄）を履かなければいけないの？

　馬は鉄でできた蹄鉄をつけたりせずに野生の世界を永いこと生きてきました。ではなぜ人は馬に蹄鉄を履かせるのでしょうか？

　答えは人類がどのようにして馬を自然の世界から連れ出してきたか、という事情と関係があるのです。馬の中には新しい食べ物のありかを見つけるために、1日に20マイルもの距離を移動するものがいるように、大自然の中で馬は自由に走り回り、つねに移動しています。こうした頻繁な移動があれば、野生の馬には強くて丈夫なひづめができます。また古いひづめは自然にすり減って、新しいものに生え変わっていきます。

　ところが、人が馬を自然界から連れ出して、人の生活様式にあわせて育てるようになりました。馬は自由に走り回ることはできなくなり、1日のうちの長い時間を畜舎の中でじっと立って過ごすようになりました。そして馬の中には舗装された道路を歩いたり走ったりすることに慣れなければならないものもいました。

Over time, domesticated horses lost their ability to grow new, strong hooves quickly. Instead, they began to have feet trouble, and walking on roads caused all kinds of problems in their bodies. So, to protect horses' feet, humans came up with the horseshoe, a thin, metal, U-shaped strip that can be nailed to a horse's hoof. This makes weak hooves stronger and prevents health problems for the horse.

Nature and Animals 自然と動物

　時間が経つと、こうして家畜化された馬は、新しい丈夫なひづめを早く生やすことができないようになってしまいました。それどころか、馬には足のトラブルが起きるようになり、道路を歩くことが馬たちのあらゆる体の変調をもたらす原因になったのです。そこで、人は馬たちの足を守るために、薄い金属製でU字形にしたものを馬のひづめに釘で打ち付ける蹄鉄という方法を発明したのです。こうして弱くなったひづめは強くなり、馬に起きていた健康上の問題は起きないようになったのです。

Why do dogs bury their bones?

If you give a dog a bone, it seems like the first thing it does is try to find the perfect place to bury it. All breeds of dogs do this, and it's the same for pet dogs as well as for wild dogs. So why do they do it? Like much of animal behavior, it has to do with evolution.

Life in the wild wasn't easy for most animals, including dogs. Food was hard to get, and animals had to fight each other for it.

When a dog killed an animal or found something to eat, it usually didn't take very long for other meat-eating animals to smell the food and come looking for it. To avoid losing its meal, a dog would bury the food as soon as it had a couple bites so the smell would be covered and the food could be saved for later.

Many animals have this same kind of "save for later" habit. Just look at beavers, squirrels, and even ants for examples of other animals that store their food.

Nature and Animals 自然と動物

犬はどうして骨を地面に埋めるの？

　犬は骨を与えられると、まず最初に骨を埋めるに最適の場所を探すようです。どんな種類の犬でもそうですし、ペットの犬だろうが野生の犬だろうが同じことです。どうして犬はこのようなことをするのでしょう？　動物の行動のほとんどがそうであるように、こうした行動は進化と関係があります。

　大自然の中での生活はどんな動物たちにとっても容易なことではありません。それは犬でも同じです。食べ物は簡単に得られないし、それを得るために互いに戦わなければなりません。

　犬がある生き物を殺したり食べ物を見つけても、たいがいすぐに他の肉食動物がそのにおいを嗅ぎつけて探しにきてしまいます。見つけた食べ物を失わないようにするために、犬はちょっとだけかじったらその食べ物を埋めてしまい、匂いを残さないようにするのです。そうすれば後のために取っておくことができます。

　多くの動物に似たような「後のために取っておく」という習慣が見出せます。食べ物を貯蔵する動物にはビーバーやリス、そしてアリなどの例があります。

Why do geese fly in a V formation?

When you look up at a group of geese flying, they seem to always travel in a V formation. Scientists say there might be two reasons for this.

Some believe that the V lets each bird take shelter from the wind by using the bird in front of it as a wind block. Others say that because birds have eyes on the sides of their head, the V formation helps them see the leader and the group much better.

Nature and Animals 自然と動物

なぜガンの群れは V字形になって飛ぶの？

　ガンの群れが飛んでいるのを見上げると、いつもV字型の編隊を組んでいるのに気づくでしょう。科学者によるとこれには2つの理由があるようです。

　1つはV字型だと前を飛んでいる鳥を風よけとして利用できるということ。他の説では鳥の目は頭の側面に付いているのでV字型の編隊だとリーダーやグループの姿を見やすい利点があると言われています。

Why can parrots talk?

Parrots can't actually talk, but they are very good at copying the sounds that they hear. Although parrots can be trained to "say" certain things, they don't actually understand the meaning of the words.

However, parrots are very social animals and they need to communicate with others in their group to stay happy and healthy. If a parrot doesn't have another parrot to communicate with, they begin to make the sounds of the other animals around them.

For pet parrots, this means making human sounds because they are surrounded by humans. In this way, the parrot feels like it is part of the group and it will feel safe and happy.

Nature and Animals 自然と動物

オウムはどうして人の言葉を話すの？

　オウムは実は話ができるのではなく、聞いている音をとても上手に真似をすることができるのです。オウムはある種の言葉を「しゃべる」ように訓練することができますが、言葉の意味を理解しているわけではありません。

　ただオウムはとても社交的な生き物で、同じ仲間のメンバーとコミュニケーションをすることで楽しく健康に生きることができるのです。もしオウムにコミュニケーションする別のオウムがいないと、周りにいる他の動物の音を真似し始めるのです。

　ペットのオウムにとっては、人の声を真似するのは人に囲まれているからです。このような方法でオウムはグループの一員と感じることができて、気持ちが休まり幸せを感じるというわけです。

Why are male animals usually more colorful than the female?

In the wild, the female of the species is usually the one who gets to select a mating partner. Males developed bright colors and features to look more attractive, and to have a better chance at being selected for mating. However, the bright colors often make males easy to see for predators.

Females, on the other hand, have dull or darker colors as a form of protection, because these dull colors let them blend into nature, making them hard to see.

Nature and Animals 自然と動物

なぜ動物の雄は雌よりも派手なの？

　自然界では、通常その種の雌が一緒になるパートナーを選ぶ立場にあります。雄はより相手の関心を惹くような派手な色や容貌でパートナーに選んでもらう機会を広げています。でも明るい色は、捕食者によっても見つけられやすいのです。

　一方、雌たちは身を守るため地味で暗めの色をしていています。こうした地味な色は自然の中にとけ込みやすく、天敵には見つけにくくなります。

Do other animals laugh when tickled?

Scientists have found that a few other animals aside from humans laugh when tickled. Several types of monkeys and rats also react to tickling with laughter. But why do we laugh when tickled? This is a much more difficult question. Scientists think it developed as a form of social connection, as well as a way for animals to get training in self-protection. You might notice that the most ticklish areas are around the ribs and belly—areas that are weak to attack.

Nature and Animals 自然と動物

動物はくすぐったいと笑うの？

　人以外で、くすぐったいと笑う動物というのがいくつかのケースで見つかっています。猿とネズミのいくつかの種ではくすぐったいときに「笑い」で反応することがわかっています。でもどうしてくすぐったいと笑うのでしょうか？　これは大変難しい問題です。研究者の中には社会的なつながりの一形態として、また同時に動物にとっては自己を防衛するためのトレーニング方法として発達させたと考える人もいます。くすぐったいと感じる箇所が肋骨と腹部の周辺であることはご存知ですよね。この辺りは敵からの攻撃に弱い場所だからです。

Why are dogs' noses wet?

Dogs' noses are wet so that they can smell things in the air better. The dog's nose produces a thin layer of wetness that helps catch the chemicals in the air that give off smells. Dogs also lick their noses often, making their noses even wetter. But the licking also helps the dog catch every possible smell in the air. By licking its nose, the dog tastes those smell chemicals and presents them to more smelling senses in the roof of its mouth. Also, the wetness of the nose is thought to help keep the dog cool, because dogs do not sweat.

Nature and Animals 自然と動物

どうして犬の鼻はぬれているの？

　犬の鼻がぬれているのはその方が空気中の匂いを敏感に嗅ぎ取ることができるからです。犬の鼻には湿り気のある薄い層があり、それが匂いの元である空気中の化学物質をとらえるのに役立っているのです。犬は鼻をもっと湿らせるためにしばしば自分の鼻をなめています。でも、なめることで空気中の匂いのすべての成分をもっと正確に把握することができます。また、なめることで匂いの成分を味わうだけでなく、それを口内の天井部分に移して、その匂いをさらに確かめるのです。さらに鼻がぬれているのは汗をかけない犬にとって体を冷やす効能もあります。

Food
食べ物

Why is Caesar salad called a Caesar salad?

The Caesar salad is named after the man who invented the recipe. Caesar Cardini was a chef who owned a restaurant called Caesar's Place in Tijuana, Mexico.

One day, a large group of tourists came into his restaurant, but he only had a few ingredients in his kitchen. Determined not to lose his customers or let them down, he created a salad with the few things he had: Romaine lettuce, anchovies, grated cheese, and croutons.

Then, for extra flavor he topped it with a salad dressing he came up with on the spot. He mixed together some egg, olive oil, lemon juice, and garlic.

The tourists happily ate their meal and the salad became famous. When it made its way into other restaurants, chefs honored the man who created the dish by naming it "Caesar's salad."

Food 食べ物

なぜシーザーサラダと呼ばれるようになったの？

　シーザーサラダの名前の由来はこのレシピを最初に作った人の名前から来ています。シーザー・カルディーニはメキシコのティフアナにあるシーザーズ・プレイスと呼ばれるレストランを経営するシェフでした。

　ある日、大集団の旅行者が彼のレストランに来ましたが、厨房にはあまりいろいろな具材がありませんでした。彼はこの団体客を失うまいと、またガッカリさせまいとして、この限られた具材からサラダを作ったのです。具材は、ロメイン・レタス、アンチョビ、粉チーズ、そしてクルトンでした。

　それからその場の即興で作り出したサラダ・ドレッシングで風味を足しました。カルディーニ氏はそのドレッシングを、卵、オリーブオイル、レモン汁、そしてニンニクを混ぜて作ったのです。

　この旅行者たちはそれを食べて満足し、このサラダは有名になりました。それが他のレストランでも採用された際、シェフたちはこのレシピを発明した彼の偉業をたたえて「シーザーサラダ」と命名したのです。

Where did the McDonald's sign come from?

The McDonald's sign, also known as the "golden arches," came from the design of the original restaurant.

The first McDonald's restaurant was built in 1953 with two yellow arches at either end of the building. The arches didn't have a purpose; they were simply there to make the building look more interesting.

But when the company decided to make a new logo in 1962, the designer came up with an "M" made of two arches that looked like the arches of the original restaurant. The "M" stood for "McDonald's" and is still used as one of the most widely recognized logos in the world today.

Food 食べ物

マクドナルドのマークは
どこから来たの？

　「ゴールデンアーチ」という名前でも知られるマクドナルドのロゴマークは、最初の店のデザインから来ています。

　1953年に建てられたマクドナルドの1号店の建物の両端には、2つの黄色いアーチがついていました。アーチ自身には特に何の目的もなく、単に建物の見栄えを面白くするだけでした。

　でも1962年にマクドナルド社がロゴを決めようとした時、デザイナーが1号店の2つのアーチに似せてMの字を図案化したものを考え出したのです。Mのロゴは「McDonald's」のMであり、世界中で誰もが知っている有名なロゴとして今でも使われているのです。

Why does popcorn pop?

Not every kind of corn will pop. Popcorn is a special type of corn called *zea mays everta*, and it is special because it has an extra-hard outer shell. This hard shell is very important to the process of popping.

To be ready for popping, a piece of popcorn has to have the right amount of water within its hard shell. When this piece of popcorn is heated, the water inside will become steam and expand.

The hard shell keeps this steam trapped inside until the pressure is so great that the shell explodes, setting the steam and starches of the corn free. When the explosion happens, the air outside the popcorn cools the starches and makes them turn solid, forming the light, white part of popcorn.

Food 食べ物

ポップコーンはどうしてできるの？

　すべてのトウモロコシがポップコーンになるわけではありません。ポップコーンは「ジーア・メイズ・エヴェルタ」という特別な種類のトウモロコシなのです。どうしてそれが特別かというと、外皮が特にかたい種類だからです。このかたい外皮がトウモロコシがポップコーン状になる過程で重要なのです。

　ポップコーンになるには、トウモロコシひとつひとつのかたい外皮の中に適切な量の水分が入っていなければなりません。こうした種類のトウモロコシが熱せられると、内側の水分が蒸発して膨張します。

　このかたい外皮は、水分とでんぷんを放出する寸前まで閉じ込めていますが、内側の蒸気の圧に耐えられなくなって破裂します。破裂すると、外側の空気ででんぷんが冷えて固まり、ポップコーンの軽くて白い部分になるのです。

Why are M&Ms called M&Ms?

M&Ms, the popular chocolate candies, are named after Forrest E. Mars and Bruce Murrie. Mars was the son of Frank C. Mars, the founder of Mars Company, a large American chocolate company. Murrie was the son of William F. R. Murrie, the president of Hershey's Chocolate, another major American chocolate company.

Forrest Mars came up with the idea for M&Ms during the Spanish Civil War in the 1930s. He saw soldiers eating chocolate with a hard shell that prevented the candies from melting. Once he was back in the United States, he told Bruce Murrie about it.

Mars and Murrie, the sons of the two biggest chocolate companies in America, decided to work together to create and sell the new candy. They decided to call the candy "M&Ms," for their last names, Mars and Murrie.

Food 食べ物

M&Msはどうして M&Ms と呼ばれるようになったの？

　大人気の大人気のチョコレート菓子「M&Ms」は、フォレスト・E・マースとブルース・マーリーにちなんで名付けられています。マース氏は、アメリカの大手チョコレート会社であるマース社の創業者創業者フランク・C・マース氏の息子でした。マーリー氏は、アメリカでもう1つの大手チョコレート会社ハーシー社の社長、ウィリアム・F・R・マーリー氏の息子でした。

　フォレスト・マース氏は1930年代のスペイン市民戦争のころM&Msのアイデアを思いつきました。彼はチョコレートが溶けないように固い殻の付いたチョコレートを食べている兵士に出くわしました。合衆国に戻ってきた時、ブルース・マーリー氏にそのことを話しました。

　アメリカ最大のチョコレート会社の2社の息子たちであったマースとマーリーが一緒に新しいお菓子を作り出し販売することを決めたのです。彼らはこのチョコレートを名字のイニシャルをとってM&Msと命名したのです。

Why is a hamburger called a hamburger?

The idea for hamburgers actually came from Central Asia. The Tartar people, who were great horse riders, traveled with meat under their saddles to make the meat tender as they rode. In the 18th century, this idea was introduced to Germans, who liked the idea of softened meat.

The Germans created their own softened meat in Hamburg, a German city, and called the dish "Hamburg steak."

Germans brought the Hamburg steak to America and the dish became an instant success. As Americans experimented with the dish, they decided to make a sandwich out of it, and this came to be known as a "hamburger."

Food 食べ物

ハンバーガーはなぜハンバーガーと呼ばれるようになったの？

　ハンバーガーの起源は中央アジアです。騎馬民族のタタール人たちは、馬で移動するあいだ、肉を鞍の下に置いて柔らかくしたのです。18世紀になってこの方法が、肉を柔らかくするのが好きなドイツ人たちに伝わったのです。

　ドイツの都市ハンブルクのドイツ人たちは肉を柔らかくする独自の方法を考えつき、それを「ハンバーグステーキ」と呼びました。

　ドイツ人たちはハンバーグステーキをアメリカにもたらし、この食べ物はただちに成功しました。アメリカ人がこれを試したとき、それをサンドイッチにして食べたので、それが「ハンバーガー」として知られることになったのです。

Why are French fries called French fries?

Most historical accounts say that the thin, deep-fried strips of potatoes we now know as "French fries" were actually invented by the Belgians. Records say that Belgians first started frying potatoes in the Meuse Valley in the 17th century.

The valley had many rivers, and it was very common for people to fry fish for their meals. But, when the rivers froze during especially hard winters, it was difficult to fish, so people would fry potatoes instead.

However, the French say they were also frying potatoes at around the same time. The potatoes became very popular and common all over France.

So, when the fried potatoes made their way to America, they became known as "potatoes fried in the French manner," and later, simply "French fries."

Food 食べ物

フライドポテトはどうして英語で「フレンチフライ」と呼ばれるの？

　歴史的記録によれば、現在「フライドポテト」として知られている薄く切って油でよく揚げた細長いジャガイモは、実はベルギー人によって発明されたそうです。記録にはベルギー人が17世紀にミューズ・バレーでポテトのフライを始めたと書いてあります。

　この谷にはたくさん川があって、住人は食事の時に油で揚げた魚をよく食べていたそうです。ところが、その川が特に厳しい冬の時期に凍結してしまい、釣りができなくなったため、その代わりにジャガイモを揚げたのだろうということです。

　しかしフランス人は同じ頃すでにジャガイモを揚げていたと主張しています。フランス中でジャガイモは人気があって一般的な食べ物だったのです。
　そんなわけで揚げたジャガイモの料理がアメリカに来た時、「フランス式の揚げジャガイモ」として知られるようになり、それが後に「フレンチフライ」と呼ばれるようになったのです。

Why do onions make your eyes water?

Cutting onions makes people cry because they contain a chemical that irritates the eyes. Like many plants in the Allium species, onions suck sulfur out of the ground. When an onion is cut, its cells break apart, releasing chemicals that mix with the sulfur and create a gas that upsets the human eye.

The burning feeling in the eyes tells the brain to produce tears, which is a way to wash away anything that upsets the eye.

Food 食べ物

なぜタマネギを切ると涙が出るの？

　タマネギを切ると涙が出てしまうのは、タマネギの中には目がきりきり沁みる化学物質が含まれているからです。アリウム（ネギ）属の多くの植物がそうであるように、タマネギは地中から硫黄成分を取り込みます。タマネギを切ると細胞がこわれて硫黄を含んだ成分が放出されて、人の目を刺激するガスが生じるのです。

　この強い刺激は脳に涙を出すように指令し、目の中に入って悪さをするものを流し落とそうとするわけです。

Why does garlic make your breath smell bad?

Garlic, like onions, is a plant of the Allium species, which takes sulfur from the soil. Sulfur has a strong smell, and when we eat it, our mouths take on the smell. In addition, the sulfur goes into our blood. The sulfur is carried through the blood into our lungs, so the smell stays on the breath even if the mouth is cleaned.

The body also tries to remove the sulfur in different ways, such as through sweat. Because of this, sometimes the whole body will smell like garlic until the sulfur makes its way completely out of the body.

Food 食べ物

ニンニクを食べると どうして息が臭くなるの？

　ニンニクはタマネギと同じアリウム（ネギ）属の植物で、地中から硫黄を取り込みます。硫黄はとても強い匂いを持った物質で、私たちがそれを食べると匂いも口の中に入ってきます。加えて、この硫黄成分は血液中にも入ってきます。これが血液を通して肺にまでやってくるので、口の中がきれいになっても匂いのもとが息の中にも留まってしまうのです。

　体はこの硫黄分を汗で出したりと、さまざまな方法で取り除こうとします。このために時として、硫黄成分が体から抜け切るまでは全身からニンニクの匂いが出てしまうこともあるわけです。

Why does Swiss cheese have holes in it?

The bacteria in Swiss cheese make the holes. The bacteria give off carbon dioxide among other gases, and these gases form bubbles in the cheese as it ages. The bubbles become pockets of air as the cheese become hard, making the holes that Swiss cheese is famous for.

Food 食べ物

スイスチーズにはどうして穴があいているの？

　スイスチーズの中のバクテリアがチーズに穴を作ります。このバクテリアは二酸化炭素その他のガスを排出します。チーズが熟成する過程でこれらのガスがチーズの中に気泡を作るのです。この気泡はチーズが固くなると空気をためる「ポケット」として残り、スイスチーズのあの有名な穴になるのです。

Why do doughnuts have holes?

There is a colorful story about why doughnuts have holes. Nobody knows if the story is true, but it's still considered a pretty good explanation of why the doughnut is such an interesting shape.

The story goes back to the year 1847, when a 16-year-old American sailor from Maine named Hanson Gregory was making doughnuts. At the time, doughnuts were not called doughnuts—they were simply called "fried cakes," or sometimes "twisters." These fried cakes had two shapes at the time: they were either cut into a diamond, or they were made into a long strip of dough that was folded in half and then twisted.

The problem with these cakes, said Gregory, was that when you fried them, the edges would get cooked thoroughly but the center would stay soft and raw. As Gregory made the cakes, he had an idea. Why not

Food 食べ物

なぜドーナツには
穴があいているの？

　ドーナツに穴があるといういきさつには実に多彩な物語が秘められています。これが本当の話かどうかは誰にもわかりませんが、ドーナツがこのような面白い形になった理由のとてもよい説明であると今でも考えられているのです。

　物語は1847年に遡ります。メイン州出身のハンソン・グレゴリーという名の16歳の船乗りがドーナツを作っていました。この時点ではまだドーナツとは呼ばれておらず、単純に「揚げケーキ」とか、時には「ツイスター」などと呼ばれていました。こうした揚げたお菓子にはそのころ2つの形がありました。ダイヤモンド型に切ったものか、「ドウ」と呼ばれる長く伸ばしたパン生地を半分に曲げるかよじった形のものです。

　グレゴリーは、こうした揚げ菓子の困ったところは、揚げた時に端の部分はよく火が通るのに、中心付近が柔らかく生のままのことがあるところだと考えていました。グレゴリーはこのケーキを作っているとき突然ひらめきました。この菓子から中心をなく

get rid of the center, so the whole cake could be fried evenly?

So Gregory picked up the round lid off of a pepper container and punched a hole out of the center of the doughnuts that he was making. He fried them up, and just like he thought, the whole cake fried nice and evenly. There was no more uncooked, raw center—only delicious, fried cake. Ever since then, doughnuts have been made with holes in the middle.

However, there is another theory. At just around the same time doughnuts were gaining popularity in America, so were bagels, which were mostly sold in New York. The bagel makers made bagels with a hole in the center so they could put them one on top of the other on a stick, like a tower. This saved space when displaying the bagels. Some people say that doughnut makers liked this idea and started making holes in doughnuts so they could be displayed the same way.

Food 食べ物

せば全体によく火が通るのではないか、と。

　グレゴリーは胡椒入れの丸い蓋を使って、作っているドウの中心に穴を開けたのです。そして油で揚げると彼が予想した通りケーキ全体にいい感じに火が通ったのです。火の通っていない生の部分がなくなって、よく揚がって美味しいところしかない揚げケーキができあがったのです。それ以来、ドーナツには中央に穴があるというわけです。

　別の説もあります。アメリカでドーナツの人気が出始めた頃、ほぼニューヨーク限定で売られていたベーグルも同時に人気が出始めていました。ベーグルメーカーは中心に穴のある形にベーグルを作っていたので、棒に通して塔のようにベーグルをどんどん重ねて置くことができたのです。これならベーグルを店頭に並べる時も場所をとらなくてすみます。人々の中にはこのアイデアをドーナツメーカーが気に入って、店頭で同じように並べるためにドーナツの中心にも穴をあけ始めたと考える人もいます。

Why do lobsters and crabs turn red when cooked?

The shells of lobsters and crabs have several different chemicals. One of the chemicals produces a red color, but it is covered by two other protein chemicals that make the shell look blue, grey, or brown. Heat destroys the blue, grey, and brown protein chemicals, allowing the red chemical to show through. So when lobsters and crabs are cooked, they turn bright red.

Food 食べ物

ロブスターやカニは
火を通すとどうして赤くなるの？

　ロブスターやカニの甲羅にはさまざまな化学物質が含まれています。そのうちの1つがこの赤い色を作り出すのですが、それは甲羅を青、グレー、あるいは茶色に見せる2つのタンパク質によって覆われているのです。熱は、青、グレー、茶色のタンパク質を破壊するため、赤い色の物質が見えてくるのです。それでロブスターやカニを調理すると、色が明るい赤に変わるのです。

Why are pancakes only eaten for breakfast?

Pancakes are delicious—so why don't people eat them at all times of the day?

Historically, in the United States, pancakes were eaten for meals all throughout the day. But the first pancakes were thin, similar to French crepes. They were perfect for eating with meaty stews and soups, because the pancakes could be used to wipe up the soup from bowls and eaten as a delicious end to the meal.

Food 食べ物

パンケーキを食べるのは
どうして朝食だけなの？

　パンケーキはおいしいですよね。だったらどうして一日中いつでも食べないのでしょうか？

　歴史的にアメリカではパンケーキは1日のうち、いつでも食べられていました。初期のパンケーキは薄く、フランスのクレープに似たもので、肉のたっぷり入ったシチューやスープと相性の良いものでした。というのはこうしたスープなどを食べ終わった後で、うれしい仕上げとして、このパンケーキを使ってお椀から残りをきれいにむだなくさらうことができたからです。

However, in the 1780s, American cooks began adding a chemical that made the pancakes thick and fluffy, similar to bread. But unlike bread, which took hours to bake, the pancake could be fried in just a few minutes. This made pancakes the perfect breakfast food because they were quick to make and filling to eat. People cooking quickly in the morning before a day of work began to make pancakes as their regular breakfast food.

But pancakes never became a dinner food, because cooks had all day long to prepare dinner. As the last meal of the day, dinner was supposed to show off the skills of the cook, so they preferred to make more difficult dishes for dinner, not the quick and easy pancake. In this way, pancakes became an appropriate food for breakfast, but not for other meals.

Food 食べ物

　ところが1780年代、アメリカ人は調理する時に、パンケーキをパンのように厚みがあって柔らかいものに変える、ある種の成分を加え始めました。作るのに何時間もかかるパンと違って、パンケーキならほんの数分で作ることができます。それでパンケーキは素早く作れてお腹もいっぱいになる理想の朝食となったのです。仕事に行く前の1日の始めに素早く朝食を作らなければいけない人々にとって、パンケーキが朝食の定番になりはじめたのです。

　でもパンケーキは料理人が1日かけて用意する夕食にはなりませんでした。1日を締めくくるディナーは、料理人が腕を振るってみせるもので、手間のかかる料理が好まれますから、素早く簡単な料理であるパンケーキは夕食にふさわしくないというわけです。こうして、パンケーキは朝食にこそふさわしいものとして考えられるようになったのです。

Why does salt bring out flavor?

Humans can recognize five different flavors: salty, sweet, bitter, sour, and *umami*. Adding salt to food not only makes the dish more salty, but it can also bring out the true flavor of the food. This is because salt helps release certain molecules into the air, and this increases the smell of the food. Smell is an important sense that is tied to taste, so if a food smells strongly, the flavor will also be stronger.

Not only that, but salt is also known to lessen the bitter taste of some foods. This helps the other flavors of the food come out. Also, when salt is added to sweet or sour things, it can help balance out these powerful flavors, allowing us to taste other, weaker flavors of the food.

Food 食べ物

食べ物は塩を足すとどうしておいしくなるの？

　人は、塩辛味、甘味、苦味、酸味、うま味という5つの味を認識することができます。塩は食べ物を単に塩辛くするだけでなく、食材の本当の味を引き出すこともできるのです。これは塩が食べ物からある種の成分を空気中に放出させるからで、食べ物の香りも高くなります。香りというのは味と結びついたとても重要な感覚のひとつで、食べ物の香りが強いほど、味も強く感じるものなのです。

　それだけではなく、塩はある種の食べ物の苦みを和らげる効果があることでも知られています。こうした効果は食べ物の隠れた味を引き出します。また、甘いものや酸っぱいものに塩が加わると、くせのある味のバランスがよくなったりするため、食べ物に隠された弱い味も感じることができるようになるのです。

Why does eating cold things give you a headache?

Have you ever noticed when drinking a glass of ice water or eating ice cream that your head starts to hurt all of a sudden? Sometimes people call this "brain freeze." What causes it?

When something cold touches the roof of your mouth, the sudden change in temperature makes your blood vessels expand. This is how your body tries to send blood to the area to warm it back up.

But the expanding of these vessels wake up nerves that sense pain, which send messages that the brain reads as pain in the forehead. This pain usually only lasts from 10 to 30 seconds, but it is a fairly common experience. About one out of three people experience this type of headache when they eat cold things.

Food 食べ物

冷たいものを食べると なぜ頭が痛くなるの？

　氷の入った水を飲んだり、アイスクリームを食べたりすると、突然頭が痛くなったことはありませんか？ 人によってはこれを「ブレイン・フリーズ」と呼んだりするようですが、なぜこれは起こるのでしょう？

　何か冷たいものが口蓋に当たると、急激な温度の変化で血管が拡張します。これは冷えた部位を温めなおすために血液を送ろうとする体の反応なのです。

　でも血管の拡張は痛みの神経を目覚めさせ脳にシグナルを送るため、額のところに痛みがあると感じるのです。この痛みは10秒から30秒ほどでおさまるもので、誰もがごく普通に経験します。およそ3人に1人は冷たいものを食べた時に同様の痛みを経験するということです。

誰かに話したくなる「世の中のなぜ？」

2015年3月1日　第1刷発行

著　者　ニーナ・ウェグナー

発行者　浦　晋亮

発行所　IBCパブリッシング株式会社
　　　　〒162-0804 東京都新宿区中里町29番3号 菱秀神楽坂ビル9F
　　　　Tel. 03-3513-4511　Fax. 03-3513-4512
　　　　www.ibcpub.co.jp

印刷所　株式会社シナノパブリッシングプレス

© IBC Publishing. Inc. 2015

Printed in Japan

落丁本・乱丁本は、小社宛にお送りください。送料小社負担にてお取り替えいたします。
本書の無断複写（コピー）は著作権法上での例外を除き禁じられています。

ISBN978-4-7946-0332-6